Alternative
to FUTILITY

Alternative *to* FUTILITY

by ELTON TRUEBLOOD

PROFESSOR OF PHILOSOPHY, EARLHAM COLLEGE

NEW YORK AND LONDON

HARPER & BROTHERS PUBLISHERS

ALTERNATIVE TO FUTILITY

FIRST EDITION

M—W

DEDICATION

To those students of Earlham who have
provided a demonstration, rather than an
argument, in support of the theme of this
book

Contents

PREFACE   9

I. BEYOND DIAGNOSIS   13

II. THE HABIT OF ADVENTURE   36

III. THE FELLOWSHIP OF THE CONCERNED   58

IV. THE RECOVERY OF DISCIPLINE   82

V. THE GRACE OF IMPATIENCE   104

Preface

Three years ago, I wrote a book in which I sought to analyze the sickness of our total civilization. In the preface to that slender volume I said, "It is the conviction of the author that the trouble we face is more profound than we normally suppose and that the solution of our difficulties will likewise lie along deeper lines than we normally suppose." Unfortunately, the evidence of the truth of the first part of this sentence has been increasingly abundant in the months that have intervened. The end of the war did not bring an end to our difficulties, because the war was more a symptom than a cause of our sickness. Indeed, there is a sense in which the war has not really ended, and in which peace has not really come. Real peace may not come in our time.

These words are being written on the anniversary of the most striking single event in recent centuries. We are, today, beginning the third year of the new and puzzling age in which it is our destiny, perhaps our tragedy, and possibly our glorious opportunity, to be alive. We dare not accept the decay of the West as the last word on the subject. We must, under God's guidance, find ways in which the spirit of man can be renewed and tragedy averted.

A good many people who read the little volume encouraged me to go farther and to deal with "the solution of our difficulties." Accordingly, I have tried to do so, and the chapters which follow are the result. Anyone who attempts to think seriously about the matter knows that the positive answer is far more difficult than is the analysis of the problem, and I offer these pages with real humility. I know the danger of giving an answer which seems too simple; I know how much easier it is to criticize than to create; I know there are churchmen who will consider my thesis too unconventional, and I know there are intellectuals who will consider it too pious. All I can say is that I have sought to give the best positive answer of which I am capable and, furthermore, that I have had the temerity to be specific rather than vague and merely general in describing the steps we must take.

Because the ideas developed in this book have dominated my thinking for the last three years, I have presented different aspects of the central thesis before various audiences in this country and abroad. Some of my readers may, therefore, feel a certain familiarity with some of the ideas as now presented. Indeed, some may recognize particular ideas as their own, for the very good reason that they *are* their own. Nearly all of the oral presentations, including those in small towns, have elicited ideas from the auditors which have been extremely helpful and which I have not hesitated to adopt. This is as it should be, for the work of the lonely thinker is a fiction. Creative thought goes forward as we learn from one another, until something like a "sense of the meeting" begins to emerge. I take this opportunity of thanking all who have contributed in this way.

My special thanks, however, go to President David Stitt,

of Austin Seminary, at whose invitation the chapters were prepared, in their present form, as a series of lectures.

The Annual Mid-Winter Lecture Series at the Austin Presbyterian Theological Seminary was instituted in 1944 in response to the expressed desire of the alumni. For three years this series was sponsored jointly by the alumni association and the seminary.

Lecturers and publications during this period are:

1944—Ernest Trice Thompson—*Christian Bases of World Order*

1945—Josef Lukl Hromadka—*Europe at the Cross Roads*

1946—Paul Scherer—*The Plight of Freedom*

In 1947, Mr. Lem Scarbrough of Austin, Texas, underwrote the 1948 lectureship. This volume, therefore, appears as the 1948 Scarbrough Lectures.

D. E. T.

Earlham College
Two years after Hiroshima

Chapter I

BEYOND DIAGNOSIS

There is only one way in which we can hope to emerge from the meaningless state in which we are now held captive into one informed with meaning.

—ALBERT SCHWEITZER

Concerning the sickness of Western man the doctors agree. During the last few years, and particularly since the conclusion of open hostilities, the reading public has been offered an abundance of studies describing various symptoms in detail. In this abundance of diagnosis there has been a remarkable meeting of minds. All who think seriously about the matter are agreed that decay has set in and they are likewise agreed, in great measure, on the reasons for this decay. There is marked similarity even in the titles of books.[1]

Important as this diagnosis is, and much as we owe to the diagnostic pioneers, such as Schweitzer and Berdyaev, our main emphasis *now* must be placed on prescription and

[1] Two recent titles are *The Annihilation of Man* and *The Abolition of Man.*

cure. We have discarded the blasphemy of optimism; we are wholly humble about our condition; but there must be some path of recovery and renewal. We are now thoroughly convinced of the truth of the first axiom of the philosophy of civilization, the axiom that, no matter how powerful a civilization may be in military strength, and no matter how rich it may be in physical resources, it *can* go down, if other conditions of survival are lacking. Since the dawn of history the truth of this axiom has been demonstrated many times and in strikingly similar ways. The decay of ancient Rome is the most familiar of these demonstrations.

It is now time to pay equal attention to the second axiom of the philosophy of civilization, the axiom that nations and peoples, even after long decay and corruption, can be revived and redirected into productive lines of human advance. *The most needful thing at this hour is the concentration of the best thought of our time on the demonstration of this second axiom.* We must use all the intelligence we can muster to try to learn what the conditions are which make for revival and then learn how to produce these conditions. Now that we have lost the delusion of health, we may be in a position to accept a cure, providing there is any wisdom pointing in this direction.

As we seek a cure, it is perfectly clear that what is needed lies in the realm of the intangibles. We need many *things,* but we need a new spirit far more, because without such a spirit the *things* we already have often become a curse rather than a blessing. Actually we are well supplied with material resources. Our shameful failure in housing comes not from any lack of clay to make the bricks; there is plenty of clay, but the will is lacking. With our present resources we could have a magnificent standard of living in a short time, if only men and women would put their backs into the undertaking with enthusiasm, vision and un-stinted loyalty; but this is what we will not do. *Our incentive is unequal to our skill.*

We realize more fully the direction from which a cure must come when we note that what we have is funda-mentally a loss of nerve, not unlike that which Sir Gilbert Murray has told us occurred in the ancient world. Today's men and women, heirs of all that science and art and re-ligion have been able to provide in the accumulation of centuries, are a bewildered and confused generation. This is true not merely of the vanquished but of a majority of the victors. It is true not merely of those who live in the cellars of bombed houses and ride in converted cattle cars; it is likewise true of those who live in steam-heated apart-ments and have been fortunate enough to purchase high-powered automobiles of the latest design.

Joy has gone out of much of our lives. Millions go through the motions as though they were waiting for a catastrophe. What we miss, almost everywhere, is the up-lifted face and the flashing eye. Men cannot live well either in poverty or in abundance unless they see some meaning and purpose in life, which alone can be thrilling.

Lacking the joy which comes from meaning and pur-pose, we turn to all kinds of wretched substitutes. Thus we cultivate the sensual arts to an absurd and revolting degree. A reasonably accurate index of our level of decadence is provided by the ubiquitous advertisements of whisky, with their emphasis on delicate shades of flavor, and by the fantastically expensive advertisements of perfume. It would appear that even sexual enjoyment is in need of some encouragement.

The growth of the sensual arts, including the marked increase in the consumption of alcohol, helps us to see what it is that modern man needs. Scientific studies of the use of alcohol, notably those carried on at Yale University, show conclusively that alcoholism is the result of spiritual lack or emptiness. Men drink to excess not so much because of the love of the drug as because of failures of personality. A man for whom life has lost its meaning turns to alcohol as a substitute, and as a temporary escape from an intolerable sense of futility. Thus alcoholism as a disease must be cured, if it is cured at all, by the provision of adequate satisfactions and significance in the personal life of the ill person. This is the chief reason why Alcoholics Anonymous have been so remarkably successful. They have sought to remove the cause rather than work on symptoms.

Bad as alcoholism may be, it is not the worst that can occur in a society suffering from a sense of futility. The deepest danger in this connection is *war*. In our efforts to build enduring peace, people of good will often go on the gratuitous assumption that most people hate war and wish to remove it from the world. We ought to be able now to see that this is a serious error in judgment. Actually most of us like war better than we like peace. We like it because it saves us from boredom, from mediocrity, from dullness. It is instructive to note that great numbers of people in Britain say openly that they look back to 1940–41 with nostalgia. Those were the days in which they really lived! There was the constant danger of invasion and all the resultant horror; there was the bombing; but there was more. People stood shoulder to shoulder, united by a common pride. They were sustained by great rhetoric and by great deeds. *Life had significance.* Now all is different. Now there is no danger, but only a constant round of petty restrictions; life has become commonplace and humdrum.

If this is true of the people of Britain it is true, in varying degrees, of other peoples of the West. The awful danger is that, in such circumstances, some men and women will turn to war as other men and women turn to alcohol. Another war would be a glorious escape for a little while. It might, in the end, destroy most of the decent life on this planet, but there would again be the thrill of a crusade; again the common man would wear a uniform and be a temporary hero; again, no matter how fantastic the national debt, money would flow freely. *The consequence is that millions will prefer war so long as they lack in their inner lives a living faith which gives significance to their existence.*

The recognition of the dangers which ensue when a sense of futility comes into men's lives sheds great light on our present industrial troubles. One of our chief failures, leading necessarily to inflation, is the constant lessening of effort together with the constant demand for higher pay at all levels. This, if it keeps on, will wreck capitalism or any other system. Much of our failure lies in the fact that we look upon the problem as primarily an economic or an industrial one. If the insight based on studies in alcoholism is a valid one, and there is much to support it, our industrial trouble may really be spiritual. The pressure for higher wages, in spite of lesser output, would then appear to arise primarily from the cultural and spiritual poverty of so many lives in our century. Men in both labor and management demand more money, and their wives stimulate them in the demand, not because their lives are full, but because they are empty. Finding no real satisfaction in our work, having no sense of achievement in the co-operative furtherance of a common end, we seek more pay in order to purchase more ostentatious cars and get our satisfactions that way. Sometimes we smile when we see dwellers in wretched hovels drive out in new Cadillacs, but our smile is a boomerang, for this juxtaposition of the hovel and the Cadillac is only an exaggerated symbol of what most of us are trying to accomplish. The bigger salaries are a form of escape, much as the alcohol is.

Our economic problem is very grave, and probably becoming even more grave, but we can be utterly sure that it will never be solved on the basis of economics alone. The Achilles' heel of our economic system is the question of incentive and this is not primarily an economic question. So long as the rank and file have a sense of futility, there will be both planned and unconscious limitation of production and consequent confusion. Our economic system is failing today because men have so largely lost incentive to achievement. And they have lost incentive because, in their entire manner of living, their psychological and spiritual needs are not fulfilled. They go back and forth to their places of employment, beget children and try to pay their bills, but they do not feel that all these details are steps toward some great and dignifying end. Even dull work, whether manual or clerical, that is intrinsically repetitive and mechanical, could be ennobling if it were seen as part of something larger, but this is precisely what we have lost.

We have not yet turned to another war as an escape from

ourselves, but we have begun to hate the Russians in a way calculated to make us forget our own failures, and we are finding various lesser ways of escape. Characteristic among these is betting. The likelihood is that there are more people betting now than at any other time in history. For some reason, it seems more possible to build greyhound tracks than to build homes for needy families. In one particular organization in the Western world there are several thousand clerks employed to handle bets on football alone.

All of this means that our central problem is moral and spiritual. The central problem is not political, for it is clear that any political system will be destroyed if the life of the citizens has lost its meaning. It will be destroyed by war if by nothing else. The problems of world government, on which so many thoughtful people pin their ultimate hope of the abolition of war, are really spiritual problems, since it is clear that there cannot be world government without world community. Given the present lack of world community, the only conceivable effective world government would be a ruthlessly totalitarian one. Moreover, the central problem is not the problem of science. Science can do wonders, but it cannot do what is required now. If we are interested in noting the limits of science, we can see a revealing example in the problem of feeding our former enemies. *If* we decide to feed them, science can be of enormous assistance. It can, among other things, provide us with hybrid seed corn and with synthetic food or drugs. But it is not by reference to science that we decide *whether* we are to feed our former enemies. That is a question of quite another kind. It is a question which concerns both mercy and justice, which constitute no part of the scientific vocabulary.

It has been popular, in some intellectual quarters, to refer to the present situation as a cultural lag in which social science and moral philosophy have not been able to keep up with natural science and, accordingly, to blame the moralists for the existence of the lag. Some have said, "See, the physical scientists have been able to make tremendous advances; the moralists are blameworthy in that they have not kept pace." The moralists, we are told, must be stupid and slow. Why don't they match the physicists in brilliance?

This conception of the relative situation as between science and ethics has a certain superficial plausibility but turns out to be almost meaningless on careful analysis. Ethics and science are not comparable or equal fields but vastly and generically different. There are four important differences between them, as follows:

1. *Science and ethics do not refer to two separate groups of men.* Science is, indeed, the work of a specialized class of workers, but ethics can never be. The moral law concerns all of us as human beings, and we are all equally responsible. There is not, in ethics, some professional class to whom we can delegate the task of renewal, as we can delegate the task of atomic fission to a specialized class. It is not the moralists who have failed to keep step, but *all of us* as men and women, and this includes the scientists as well as anybody else.

2. *Both science and ethics deal with laws, but they deal with laws in radically different ways.* Science deals with laws in the sense of what actually occurs. It is therefore fundamentally descriptive. Ethics, on the other hand, deals with laws in the sense of *what ought to occur,* which is a very

different matter. The former is obviously easier to handle than is the latter, and requires a different discipline.

3. *Science and ethics are not comparable or equal realms because one of them is forced to deal with freedom while the other is not.* The materials which the ordinary scientist handles may be difficult in many ways but, in any case, they are not free to act on the basis of choice, whereas, in the reconstruction of the moral life, we are always dealing with freedom in this important sense. It cannot, therefore, be reasonably supposed that equal intelligence would give comparably neat results in the two fields.

4. *Finally, the two fields are different in that one of them must face the stubborn fact of sin.* No matter how perplexing problems in physics, chemistry or even biology may be, they are all elementary when compared with those dealing with the human heart and its amazing capacity for self-deception. We are more successful in building bridges than in building a good society because bridges are easier to build.

When we realize that we are faced with something far more profound than a "cultural lag" we are better prepared for the future. We then know very well that no amount of intelligence will give us the certainty of a good world, even though a modest amount of intelligence *will* give us excellent science. There will be self-centered men in any society. But, knowing this, we are not thereby stopped in our efforts to discover and effect a cure. We can well believe that every great burst of new life is God's doing, but we can at least be wise enough to know that there are some lines along which the divine renewal is more likely to come than others. What we must do is to observe history carefully and see whether we can discern the ways in which the probability of new life is increased.

What we seek is a situation in which the rank and file of our people are filled with a vibrant faith. If they could believe greatly in something, if they could see some purpose to give them a reason for striving, life might become more radiant than we can now imagine. Then, in spite of rubble and lack of housing, men could live joyously and victoriously. There are two chief ways in which spiritual solidarity comes, one temporary and the other enduring. The temporary way is by response to a common danger. We see this vividly in time of flood or fire. An entire community, when seriously threatened, will work together, temporarily neglecting all divisions of party or ancestry. Later we usually look back on such times as high moments, but the tragedy lies in the fact that the experience is so truly momentary. As soon as the source of danger is removed the old life returns with its divisions and its animosities. This is, therefore, no enduring way.

We are experiencing today a species of unity based on fear of communism, but this, though it involves some hysteria, is bound to fail as a basis of living. It will fail because it is based on danger rather than on a positive cause. It is almost purely negative, and a negative basis of unity, though powerful for a time, is never enduring.

The other way in which there can be spiritual solidarity is by common devotion to a great cause. This is frequently not so exciting in the beginning, but it involves remarkable endurance and releases deep springs of power. It is, ultimately, the only true way in which men can be united and inspired. If we can find a sufficiently positive cause to inspire men's loyalty, and if we can present it in such a way that millions are committed to it, we shall be on our way toward a cure for the sickness of Western man. What Western man needs more than anything else is a restoration of faith in something which will dignify his existence. This is the way of salvation. But *how* is this to be achieved and *to what* shall we be committed?

There have been, within our lifetime, two remarkable attempts to provide for the rank and file of men a sense of meaning in life and, if we are wise, we shall observe these most carefully. One of them has already ended in disaster, but the other is stronger than ever before and is daily becoming stronger. These are, as everyone knows, nazism and communism. We tend to suppose that we have heard about these sufficiently, just as we suppose that we have heard sufficiently about the atomic bomb, but in both instances we are wrong in our judgment. We may have heard enough about these two systems in the spirit of denunciation, but we have not heard enough about them in an attempt to understand the mysteries of the human spirit. Both are remarkably revealing about man—and revealing in a similar way.

The nazi system is revealing in that it shows what miracles can be wrought by a people possessed of a burning faith, even when it is a fantastically evil and monstrous faith. In 1933 the Germans were still a beaten people. Their military forces had suffered one of the greatest defeats of history; they had lost their colonies, and their navy had been sunk. "The truth is," said Lloyd George to Lord Riddell at Versailles, "that we have got our way. We have got most of the things we set out to get. . . . The German navy has been handed over, the German merchant shipping has been handed over, and the German colonies have been given up. One of our chief trade competitors has been crippled." Now the amazing thing is that a people thus crippled could revive their economy and their industry so rapidly. We know how long it takes us now to achieve even a modest recovery and *we* are victors, whereas those who listened to the nazi creed were the vanquished. Within about six years[2] after the seizure of power by the new system, Germany was ready to challenge the world, and then, for six more years, she was able to continue fighting with a large part of the industrial and military power of the world against her. This amazing exploit was accomplished by a people occupying a territory roughly equal to that of Texas.

How did the nazis perform this feat? Their chief success was in the building of morale, and this they did by the inculcation of a faith. The system of thought caught the imagination of millions because it dignified their lives by including them in a significant solidarity. The beaten and impoverished German *Volk* were not, Hitler said, what they appeared superficially to be, but were really carriers of a noble tradition. They were people whom even the proud Romans could not conquer in ancient times. The Germans, the doctrine continued, were a *Herrenvolk;* they were really a noble people already, if only they could become conscious of their high destiny.

That this doctrine had unspeakably evil consequences in the treatment of supposedly lesser peoples is well known. It led to some of the worst cruelty and horror which the

[2] According to William L. Shirer, writing in the *Atlantic Monthly* for July, 1947, the German leaders actually felt ready in October, 1938, and were not carrying through a colossal bluff, as has been generally supposed.

members of the human race have ever experienced, so that for centuries the names Dachau and Belsen and Buchenwald will be words of reproach and names such as Streicher and Goebbels will bring nausea. But what we tend to forget is the electric effect which this doctrine had on the average German, particularly on the young German. The doctrine seemed to give meaning to history; it gave the individual, no matter how humble, a part in something grand. Thus it strengthened purpose, brought joy and changed loiterers into vigorous workers or disciplined soldiers. This should be pointed out, not to excuse the system, for it was and is inexcusable, but to provide us with relevant data concerning the ways in which the spirit of man can be renewed. If there could be some way of producing this electric effect on human life without the attendant hatred and horror, we should be wise to employ it as rapidly as possible. The average life of the West is today relatively free from the horror, but we are lacking in the spirit as well.

The nazi system has fallen into general disrepute, partly because it eventually failed in a military way, but we can be sure that we have not heard the last of it. The doctrine is so attractive to so many minds, providing such a short cut to a sense of dignity in life, that we can expect it to arise again in various subtle disguises. But, meantime, there is another system, still flushed with victory, which has much the same spiritual effect in a different way. In the communist faith there is also an appeal to the poor and the downtrodden. The doctrine holds that, poor as the workers may seem, their present disability is only temporary. They are actually participants in a dialectical process which is destined to elevate them and lower their capitalistic competitors. This is not a dream, the ideology states, but a scientific fact as demonstrable as the laws of motion. The mills of history are grinding out the inevitable event, and no individual or nation can stop them. The poor workers are thus actors in a cosmic drama. In another figure, they are riding the wave of the future, which no man can hasten and no man can stay. The rise of the proletariat is impossible to stop since the drama is on a cosmic scale, rooted in the nature of things.

This system, too, involves great evils. Often it makes for a wholly ruthless spirit and political intransigence. In most instances it involves a denial of freedom, in the sense of political freedom or freedom of expression. Even the editors of newspapers are civil servants and necessarily represent the views of the one existent political party. The ugly features, involved in what is called a police state, seem to be inherent in the system. But it is clear that there are millions of individuals who accept these evils gladly because the theory so dignifies their lives. They are part of something big; they are coming into their inheritance; they are fulfilling their destiny. And, accordingly, they will work long hours, fight in the bitter cold and undergo all hardships. Their creed is manifestly an inadequate one, but we should be stupid indeed were we to allow this fact to blind us to the remarkable lift which the creed introduces into common life. We have the freedom of expression, but we do not have the *lift*.

Where shall we find the lift we so sorely need? We shall not find it by the gospel of anticommunism, especially when joined with dollar diplomacy. Such a combination has aroused some passing enthusiasm, but it is manifestly incapable of doing for us what we most need. We cannot long be united or inspired by a negative position. Hitler's standing was probably improved, in some German circles, by his anti-Jewish and anti-Russian crusades, but these could not have succeeded alone. In so far as they did succeed, it was because they provided negative corollaries of a positive doctrine, the doctrine of innate Teutonic nobility.

Granted that anticommunism is too purely negative to provide us with an adequate basis for a reviving faith, do we have any positive doctrines in the Western world? An affirmative answer seems to be indicated, in both Britain and America, if we fasten attention on economic doctrines. In Britain there are a good many who adhere zealously to the mild socialism now represented by the government, while in America there are a good many who are deeply loyal to what is called "free enterprise." Important as these loyalties may be, they will not suffice. They will not suffice because they are too purely economic, and because man cannot live by economics alone. It appears that the majority of people in both countries are almost wholly unmoved by the current economic faiths. While a few are deeply concerned over socialism or capitalism, the average man gives his first attention to next week's football pool or to the World Series, with perhaps a passing grumble about rising prices. Mere economic theory does not touch him, but it is he who must be touched if we are to overcome the sense of futility from which Western man is suffering.

What the average man needs is a religious faith or something like it. Herein has lain the crucial effectiveness of the two systems which have conducted vast laboratory experiments in our time. Both have had the wisdom to be quasireligious, in that they have dignified the individual's life by

reference to something great and noble beyond himself.
Both have transcended subjectivism by reference to a cosmic
order. Both have grounded individual dignity in a vast sweep
of history. Both have been successful in practice, because
they have had the courage to be philosophical or even metaphysical in doctrine. There is not much probability that any
system will succeed, anywhere in the world, unless it follows
a similar procedure. What we seek is a way of following this
procedure without attendant evils such as war and race
prejudice and concentration camps. We seek a faith which
can dignify the average little life by grounding it in essential bigness, but without divisiveness of class, race or nation.
If modern man can achieve a faith which gives his efforts
cosmic significance, plus universalistic sympathies, we may
have a new world. We *could* rebuild this planet as rapidly
as the Germans rebuilt their little land in the thirties. There
have been periods when a vigorous faith has swept like a
prairie fire. It is this, and no less than this, which our sagging
age requires. But the burning faith might do more harm
than good if it were not a faith which involved "liberty and
justice for all."

Once, long ago, there was such a faith and it swept the
ancient world with remarkable speed. It began in such a
modest manner, in such an out-of-the way place, that the un-
biased observer, at the beginning, would have considered
any suggestion of its success a fantastic proposition. Once
there were a few unlettered men in an obscure province, and
their movement was obviously a failure; for their Leader
had been executed! Yet something so remarkable happened
that, within a generation, these men and others like them
were beginning to make a difference in the entire Hellenic-

Roman world. They brought to a civilization suffering from a sense of futility a genuine lift and, finally, when the Roman power fell into decay, they provided the main structure of faith upon which civilization could be rebuilt.

If we ask how this most remarkable of the miracles of history was performed, we are amazed at the simplicity of the method. The world needed a saving faith and the formula was that such a faith comes by a particular kind of fellowship. Jesus was deeply concerned for the continuation of his redemptive work after the close of his earthly existence, and his chosen method was *the formation of a redemptive society.* He did not form an army, establish a headquarters or even write a book. All he did was to collect a few unpromising men, inspire them with the sense of his vocation and theirs and build their lives into an intensive fellowship of affection, worship and work. "Above everything that Jesus said or did," writes a famous Beecher Lecturer, "this stands as his supreme achievement, that he formed an organic community to carry forward in history the revelation of God, which had been made in Israel."[3]

One of the truly shocking passages of the Gospel is that in which Jesus indicates that there is absolutely no substitute for the tiny redemptive society. If this fails, he suggests, all is failure; there is no other way. The Sermon on the Mount is largely directed to making the little band understand this momentous fact, and to prepare for the consequent burden by adequate discipline. Here the key passage is the metaphor of salt. He told the little bedraggled fellowship that they were actually the salt of the earth and that,

[3] Charles Clayton Morrison, *What Is Christianity?* Willett, Clark and Company, Chicago, 1940, p. 108.

if this salt should fail, there would be no adequate preserva-
tive at all. He was staking all on one throw.

That these unqualified words were addressed to a small
group is part of our amazement, especially when we know
how weak and fallible its members were. The group at that
time included Judas, who turned out to be a traitor, Peter,
who showed himself a coward, and the sons of Zebedee,
who were crudely ambitious of personal advancement.
Sometimes we picture the Sermon on the Mount, which is
the charter of the redemptive society, as being given to a
great crowd, but the New Testament distinctly says otherwise. "And seeing the multitudes, he went up into a mountain; and when he was set, his disciples came to him: and he
opened his mouth and taught them saying, . . . Ye are the
salt of the earth."

It is good to remember that the revolutionary fellowship,
of which we read in the New Testament, was a result of
careful thought and much disciplined dreaming. In one
sense the entire burst of new life was undoubtedly the work
of God, a gift of divine grace, like the spirit which bloweth
where it listeth; but in another sense the work and thought
of dedicated men were required. Not only are the major
portions of the Gospels devoted to the careful elaboration
of this intensive fellowship but, likewise, the Epistles of St.
Paul involve many contributions to the general problem.
The Pauline Epistles are given over, in considerable measure, to creative thought about what the nature of a redeem-
ing fellowship might be. In letter after letter the same criteria appear. The fellowship must be marked by mutual
affection of the members, by a sense of real equality in spite
of difference of function, by inner peace in the face of the

world's turmoil and by an almost boisterous joy. The members are to be filled, not with the intoxication of wine, but wth that of the Spirit. Such people could hardly avoid, as the sequence in the fifth chapter of Ephesians suggests, breaking out in psalms and hymns. In the early Christian community the people sang, not from convention, but from a joy which overflowed. Life for these people was no longer a problem to solve but a glory to discern.

We are so hardened to the story that it is easy for us to forget how explosive and truly revolutionary the Christian faith was in the ancient Mediterranean world. The Church at first had no buildings, no separated clergy, no set ritual, no bishops, no pope, yet it succeeded in turning life upside down for millions of unknown men and women, giving them a new sense of life's meaning and superb courage in the face of persecution or sorrow. It is our tragedy that we are living in a day when much of this primal force is spent. Our temper is so different that we hardly understand what the New Testament writers are saying. Once a church was a brave and revolutionary fellowship, changing the course of history by the introduction of discordant ideas; today it is a place where people go and sit on comfortable benches, waiting patiently until time to go home to their Sunday dinners.

The idea of a redemptive fellowship, so amazingly central to Christianity, involves an entire philosophy of civilization. How is civilization changed? It is changed, early Christianity answers, by the creation of fellowships which eventually become infectious in the entire cultural order. We are surprised to see how little the early Christians dealt with current political and economic problems, if we may judge by the extant literature of the period. They did not even attack slavery, iniquitous as it must have been. They just went on building the kind of fellowship which was bound, eventually, to destroy slavery. All this seems alien to our modern mentality, but it may involve divine wisdom. In any case, we should not be too proud to try, for we are not doing so well on our present line of endeavor. It helps our modesty to realize that these ancient men were accused of turning the world upside down, whereas no one would accuse us of anything similar. Instead of turning the world upside down, we feel helpless as we watch the rising spiral of inflationary prices, observe with some foreboding the actions of little men in Washington and go to the races.

The sense of membership in a redemptive society would dignify individual lives in that it would give meaning to history, along with a sense of human solidarity, since membership involves men in a longitudinal, as well as latitudinal, fellowship. There has been an enduring and continuous community, beginning with a suppressed people who were preserved through all kinds of danger for the sake of a divine purpose which was destined to include all humanity. The heroes and prophets of this tradition may be spiritual ancestors of us all regardless of our biological inheritance. The story is a very old story, with a historical dialectic of its own. Glorious as Israel was, it required both transcendence and fulfillment in the formation of another community, equally dedicated, but by no means limited to one nation or race, and thus universal. Early Christians were thrilled as they thought of themselves as part of this emerging divine purpose. They had a link with eternity because in their fellowship they were partners in the creative love that made the world.

It is perfectly clear that the same method could be effective again, if we could have the simplicity to try it. Men who are partners in the redemptive task of God Himself have all the dignity of personal life that is required to lift them out of mediocrity, but their glorification does not come at the expense of others or by means of antagonism. It was a cardinal point in the redemptive fellowships which changed the ancient world that all human barriers must be transcended. There is no longer Jew or Gentile, no longer bond or free. The work is grounded in history, quite as truly as is the work of the convinced Nazi or the convinced Communist, but it involves no struggle against other races or other classes. It takes man as man, wherever he may be, and binds him into a loving fellowship which acknowledges Jesus Christ as the Lord of Life and which believes that humble men and women may be partners of the divine will. Their creed is summarized by the conviction that "In all things, God works for good *with* them who love him."

This faith is accepted intellectually and formally by millions in the modern world, but it has not caught the imagination of more than a very few. The United States of America is often mentioned as a Christian nation, but on any normal day of worship there are at least one hundred million citizens of this nation who are totally unconcerned. This might not be so discouraging if there were a vigorous remnant of committed souls, but the sobering fact is that much of the salt has already lost its savor.

What we require is not intellectual theorizing or even preaching but a *demonstration*. It is not enough to say simply, "Turn to Christ and all is well." There is only one way of turning loyally to Christ and that is by trying to create the kind of fellowship which He required of His followers. Abstract or unembodied Christianity is a fiction. *If any man says he loves God and yet loves not the brethren he is a liar!* "The revelation was not first given and afterward a community created to proclaim it," says Morrison. "The creation of the community was itself the revelation of the activity of God."[4] We cannot revive the faith by argument, but we might catch the imagination of puzzled men and women by an exhibition of a Christian fellowship so intensely alive that every thoughtful person would be forced to respect it. The creation of such a fellowship is the argument that can count in the confused world of our day. If again there appears a fellowship of men and women who show, by their vitality and moral sensitivity and overwhelming joy, that they have found something so real that they no longer seek means of escape, the seekers will have something to join without disappointment and without embarrassment. If there should emerge in our day such a fellowship, wholly without artificiality and free from the dead hand of the past, it would be an exciting event of momentous importance. A society of loving souls, set free from the self-seeking struggle for personal prestige and from all unreality, would be something unutterably precious. A wise person would travel any distance to join it. This, and this alone, will take us beyond diagnosis to cure.

The way in which a humble yet leavening fellowship may be created and guided is a question of the utmost difficulty, as it is a question of the utmost importance. It is far more difficult than are most scientific problems, because it deals with more imponderables. Consequently, wisdom in this

[4] *Ibid.,* p. 129.

field, like wisdom in any *important* field, can come only by a combination of careful intelligence and creative imagination. It is this to which we should now give our nights and days, and to which we *shall* give our nights and days, if we care greatly about the fate of the human race at this juncture.

Chapter II

THE HABIT OF ADVENTURE

Without adventure civilization is in full decay.
—ALFRED NORTH WHITEHEAD

We now have a clue which may guide us in the recovery of a sense of meaning in our lives. We find this clue in the concept of faith through a special kind of fellowship. It is something which was once proposed, once tried and once found to succeed. That it succeeded so abundantly is our chief basis of hope, because there is reason to believe that *what has been can again be.* In our dire extremity, marked especially by a sense of futility, we are justified in turning with hope to the most striking example of spiritual revival which the history of the world can show.

In turning to this example we need to remind ourselves again that that with which we are dealing is sober history. The redemptive effect of the little Christian community on the ancient civilized world is no fairy story. It is not a fantastic tale produced by an imaginative writer; it is not a philosophy of civilization which some thinker constructed in the privacy of his study; *it occurred.* Conscious of a divine destiny and filled with love of the brethren, the little groups, once established at Philippi, Corinth and Ephesus, finally altered the structure and tone of ancient culture.

Here then is our clue. The method which succeeded before must be tried again and we must not be dismayed by its amazing simplicity. The best chance for the renewal of the human spirit in the twentieth century, as in the first, lies in the formation of genuinely redemptive societies in the midst of ordinary society. Such fellowships could provide a sense of meaning for the members within the societies and, at the same time, maintain an infectious influence on the entire culture outside. This is what occurred magnificently in the first century of our era and has occurred in lesser ways in other centuries, whenever really powerful forms of fellowship arose, as in the case of the early Franciscan societies of the thirteenth century or the early Quaker societies of the seventeenth century. Our task now is to repeat the miracle of history. It seems unfortunate that so heavy a burden should rest on an instrument so fragile, but there is no other way. *That is the kind of world ours is.*

The thoughtful reader is bound, at this point, to raise an important and valid query. Was not the redemptive society of Hellenistic culture simply the Church, and is not the Church still with us? How, then, can we suggest that such a society is what our sagging culture needs for its renewal? We find churches on thousands of street corners in our great cities and at country crossroads, but the world does not seem to be saved by them. These societies, claiming loyalty to the Kingdom of God as interpreted by Jesus Christ, have had increasing opportunities for effectiveness, but the doldrums of the Western world actually get worse rather than better.

It is absurd, on the face of the matter, to say that our civilization can be renewed by a redemptive society when that is what we have already had for centuries. When the patient is getting sicker, it is ridiculous to prescribe more of the same old medicine which he has been taking for years.

This is a serious query and it deserves a serious answer. That it represents the honest misgivings of millions in the Western world there is no doubt. To answer it, no matter how modestly, requires more careful analysis of the Church as we know it and of its influence on our total civilization. The life of the Church as we know it in the Western world provides abundant reason for both discouragement and hope. Since it is so popular to engage in negative criticism of the Church, we shall do better to begin with the hope.

After all the familiar criticisms have been leveled at the existent churches, the fact remains that periods of crisis often reveal real differences between the Church and the surrounding world. The Church is divided, as other organizations, such as parties and clubs, are divided, but with the enormous difference that millions of church members consider their division a scandal and are trying mightily to do something about it, whereas divisiveness outside seems perfectly normal. The Church often reflects the ordinary standards of the world, but in many heartening cases it represents a different and far more humane standard. A striking example of this was provided during the late war, when American citizens were forcibly removed from their homes in Pacific coast states because they were of Japanese ancestry. All are now enabled to know how exceedingly unjust and how unnecessary this action was, inasmuch as the Congressional inquiry has failed to find a single authenticated case of sabotage by these people. Many suffered severe economic loss, disruption of careers and of schooling, in addition to the psychological harm of being treated as third-class citizens. A large proportion of our population knows this now, but the point is that those who knew it at the time, and had the courage to say so, were people whose idealism had been mediated to them through the fellowship which began long ago in the mind of Christ. A representative body of Japanese-Americans has recently reported, to their amazement, that all the people who helped them in relocation or education or care of property were acting from definite Christian inspiration. *The patriotic societies did not help them, but the Christian societies did.* Such an example is good to remember when criticism is most sweeping and vicious.

Another relevant example concerns relief. The Church World Service Fund and the heavy contributions through the American Friends Service Committee are well known, but the point becomes clearer if we refer to a local community. The citizens of one small and relatively poor county in Indiana have recently sent 1,000 lbs. of dried milk to the people of Austria. Those who made possible this considerable gift have never, so far as they know, seen any of the recipients. Most of the residents of the little Indiana county are Protestants whereas nearly all the recipients are Roman Catholics. What caused this odd behavior? The whole endeavor was the result of the dedicated effort of the members of two or three little churches.

Many more such relevant examples might be given to show that the censorious critics of the Church often speak in ignorance. But, having said this, we must go on to say that the causes of discouragement are both numerous and great.

Almost any thoughtful person is quick to realize that mere individual religion is insufficient, and that a fellowship is required for the maintenance of man's spiritual structure; but the *ecclesia* to which he turns so hopefully may turn out to be disappointingly *ersatz*. The "sacred fellowship" may be so taken up with struggles for institutional prestige and personal power that the honest seeker is disgusted. There is no denying that many of the best people are outside the churches precisely because they *are* the best people. The fact that they have been disgusted is something in their favor; at least it shows that their standards are encouragingly high.

A pagan civilization in the modern world or even a purely secular civilization will fail, but a man may know this and yet be unattracted by what he finds when he turns to the church near his home. He is alienated, not by the fact that it demands so much, but by the fact that it demands so little. What we require is a saving vision, but there is a deep-seated conviction among our neighbors that the experts don't know, any better than do the amateurs, how the job is to be done. Thousands think of churches as stuffy places, concerned with respectability and the conventions but with no conceivable part in the creation of courage and adventure and joy. Many of those who thus judge the Church from the outside are both incorrect and uncharitable in their judgments, but there is enough truth in what they say to make their judgment profoundly disquieting.

How disquieting the situation is may be shown in a pertinent illustration. A prominent physicist, long head of his department in a well-known American university, recently did some hard thinking on the problem of spiritual reconstruction. He came, finally, to two important conclusions:

a. We cannot have a decent world merely by scientific endeavor. In addition we must have deep moral convictions and a living religion to sustain them.

b. There can be no living religion without a fellowship. Because mere individual religion is parasitic, there must be a church or something like it, and people who care about the fate of our civilization will join it.

With these conclusions in mind the physicist set out to attend church in the town where his research was going forward. The first attempt was disappointing, so he tried another kind of church the next Sunday, but it was equally disappointing. He had gone with high hopes and after rigorous thought, but of course his fellow worshipers could not know that this was the case. It seemed to him that these people were merely going through the motions, that they did not mean what they said, that the gospel was to them an old record, worn smooth with much playing. Here, said the physicist, was a world on the very brink of a new hell, and these people had no sense of urgency or of power. The scientist had hoped that at least the sermons would speak to his condition, but they did not. Both seemed trivial. What should he do next?

In the Western world there are two main alternatives presented to the average seeker, Protestantism and Catholicism. *The tragedy is that millions find satisfaction in neither.* The evidence for this observation is provided in numerous ways, one of these being the remarkable growth of new cults and movements. Though Protestantism is still the dominant

form of Christianity in Anglo-Saxon and Scandinavian countries, and though it has provided, through the sense of personal responsibility which the open Bible gives, a sounder
basis of democracy than has any alternative faith so far
known, its hold on the average man is manifestly lessened.
Millions who formerly would have found their chief fellowship in some Protestant church now find it in the service
club, the labor union, the Parent-Teacher Association, the
Grange and the learned society. These are not, in theory,
opposed to the Church, but in practice they become actual
alternatives. Many of these fellowships seem to the people
in them to be more meaningful and rewarding, or even more
demanding, than is the fellowship of the little church around
the corner.

Much has been made, in recent years, of the divided state
of Protestantism, but this is not the most serious feature of
the situation. The divided state of Protestantism is being
overcome with remarkable rapidity. Not only are church
bodies, which number adherents in the millions, being joined
organically but, what is more significant, there is a horizontal fellowship in existence which transcends all barriers.
There is no way of knowing how large this existential horizontal fellowship is, but we know it is very large. Those
who are censorious about the divided state of Protestantism
reveal that they are out of date, often being unaware of the
actual existence of the World Council of Churches. Indeed,
the serious division is not between Protestant groups but
rather between Roman Catholicism and all other forms of
Christianity.

The basic defect of the Protestant churches lies not in their
divided condition but in their *insipidity*. They show so little

imagination. The same kind of dull and lifeless service is repeated endlessly, whatever the occasion. We are in a time of crisis when we need a dynamic fellowship to turn the world upside down; what we are offered is a stereotype. A man, having become convinced that we are in a race with catastrophe, may seek the very bread of life, but in practice he is forced to sing sentimental songs with words he does not mean, listen to some comforting platitudes and finally shake the minister's hand at the door, because there is no other way of escape. In short, this kind of church illustrates Professor Whitehead's famous dictum perfectly. It is in full decay because it lacks the element of adventure. It is not the adventurous fellowship which can redeem society. It is something else.

If Protestantism is uninviting to the average seeker, Catholicism is equally so. Though there have been some highly publicized conversions of the rich and socially prominent to the Roman church, this does not mean that the modern seeker is finding his answer in that quarter. The Roman Catholic church is repellent to millions of moderns because of its admitted exclusiveness. The thoughtful seeker has an object lesson before him in the recent experience of Spain, where he sees religious totalitarianism in practice. Intelligent lovers of freedom are not likely to forget the terms of the concordat between Mussolini and the Vatican. Freedom of worship is prized as one of the four freedoms, but anyone who can read or observe knows that the Catholic church does not really believe in freedom of worship. The clearly stated theory is that outsiders are heretics and that it is wrong to give freedom to error. The logical difficulty in this line of argument is that it assumes the possibility of human inerrancy in distinguishing between truth and error. That truth is objective we do not doubt, but there is good reason to doubt that absolute truth on any subject is vouchsafed to finite man. Because the whole truth is not likely to be contained in any one institution, any human group *can* be wrong, and exclusive claims have no bearing on an inescapable human predicament. Nobody has all the keys there are.

In actual practice the Roman church is very far from original Christianity. There was, in the beginning, no pope and not even any sharp distinction between clergy and laity. Whatever the words to Peter about the keys meant, the use of this proof text today to uphold the papacy involves a *non sequitur.* The logical leap from the fisherman of Galilee to the ruler of the Vatican is truly immense. To say that there was a leader of the apostles is one proposition, but to say that there should be a single head of all Christians in the twentieth century is a proposition of quite another order.

The chief failure of the Roman church is not the Protestant failure of insipidity but the Roman failure of bigotry. The early Christian society was humble and often had no property at all; today there are "princes of the church," vast investments and ostentatious grandeur in thousands of cities. This intentional impressiveness is a far cry from the simplicity of Christ. The heresy of Rome is that it is fundamentally self-regarding. It is more concerned with the success of an institution than with the creation of a simple redemptive fellowship. Its heresy is that it identifies too simply a fallible and proud human institution with the Kingdom of God.

Where, then, shall modern man turn, if the two chief

forms of spirtual fellowship in the Western world are so unsatisfactory, in spite of their many glories? We might make up some new religion, composed of parts of many, and representing all world faiths, but this has been tried before and has always failed. An artificially constructed faith can never succeed. Fortunately, however, a better way is available. In the spirit of adventure, and by the use of disciplined imagination, we might be able to encourage a new growth, *within the existent churches*. We might be able to inaugurate a redemptive movement that could take our dry bones and make them live. This was Ezekiel's dream long ago,[1] when the sacred fellowship was trying to sing the Lord's song in a strange land, and one result was the high inspiration of the unknown singer whom we call the Second Isaiah.

The ideal would be a reformation *within* the Church, not a reformation *from* the Church. We must nourish new shoots in the old stump. Otherwise we merely become schismatic again and dissipate our power. We have a timeless gospel, but much of its exciting appeal is lost on millions in our day. What we require, then, is a new reformation, but not one like that of the sixteenth century, which divided Christians so sharply. We need a reformation which unites at a deep level.

If we are agreed that a saving faith comes by a special kind of infectious fellowship, we can concentrate on the problem of the formation of such fellowships. In order to think productively on this problem we must combine an appreciation of past models with real boldness of mind concerning the possibilities of novelty. This is the method that

[1] Ezekiel 37:1–14.

has been so successful in producing the present burst of life in architecture—one of the accepted gains of our distraught time. It is the combination of fidelity with boldness which succeeds. Boldness alone tends to produce the merely bizarre, while exclusive respect for ancient models produces the merely quaint and antiquarian, but the combination of the two may be genuinely creative.

This principle may be applied to the formation of many different kinds of societies and is particularly applicable to the reconstruction of a college. Many are trying seriously to rebuild educatonal institutions, to make them contribute the maximum to our present culture, but they will not be effective unless they combine both filial respect and adventure. An administration will fail if it concerns itself exclusively with the experience of an earlier day, without any introduction of appropriate novelty, and it will likewise fail if it concerns itself with a wholly new curriculum and organization, without respect for what has been tested through several generations or even centuries.

Now our paramount task is to apply this principle to the formation of effective redemptive societies in our time. To do so we must observe and we must dream, and we must do both at the same time. We must analyze former experiments in creative Christian fellowship and, in many cases, we must conduct our own modest experiments. We note that the tide of spirit and life has been much higher in some centuries and in some situations than it has been in others. Why is this? What makes a creative fellowship so different from others which may be far larger and more grand? What were the principles which made the fellowships at Philippi and Corinth and Ephesus so powerful? What was it that Ignatius

Loyola included in his societies that made them so different in effectiveness from other societies of his time? What was the secret of the little bands of changed men nourished by John Wesley in Bristol and other cities? If these should appear, upon analysis, to have some factors in common, in spite of diversity of setting and leadership, such factors would deserve to be studied with unusual care. We must do the same in regard to the fresh movements of our own time, never allowing unconventionality to blind us to worth.

The major danger is not that we shall fail to appreciate past models but that we shall lack the courage to be sufficiently bold in our creative dreaming. Our tendency is to be as unimaginative as were the early designers of automobiles, who could not realize that they were dealing with something more than buggies and accordingly employed the familiar dashboard, including even the whipsocket in extreme instances. It is so much easier just to go through the familiar motions, but that is the sure recipe for failure. In this connection we can learn from a parable provided by a modern industrial process. In one of the leading chemical plants of the world the laboratory scientists have decided that they must do something truly radical about the production of film. The industry has been making small annual improvements in the making of film for many years, but now the research scientists have decided that this is not good enough. They believe that, so long as they make small improvements, they may be missing something fundamental. Accordingly, their present procedure is to go back to the original reaction and try deliberately to forget what was done last year or the year before that. They believe that, by going back to the original chemical reaction and using disciplined imagination as though entering on the quest for the first time, they may be able to make some revolutionary discoveries.

What we require is the same courage in trying to see what a church might be. Fortunately we know something about the original reaction; amazing things might occur to us if we could view it afresh. We should not then despise our fathers or our fathers' fathers but should seek to get as close as possible to the reality of which their particular societies were distant reflections. Of course neither we nor the chemists can succeed wholly in going behind accepted procedures, but it is nevertheless worth while to try. *Columbus did not succeed in reaching China, but he found America.*

There will be some chance of our success if we consciously foster the habit of adventure. When we think about the matter carefully, we begin to realize that this is the only rational way to live. Our world must have in it millions of glorious possibilities which we have not realized. The Lord has more truth to break forth from His holy Word. That significant advances in every line of human achievement are possible we cannot doubt, especially when we observe the surprising bursts that have already occurred in our history. But, by the same token, we can go backward, and there have been some surprising reversals in recent times. The one thing we cannot do is to stand still. Those who suppose they have reached perfection, and then seek to maintain it, always discover in time that they have lost it. In one of the most exciting passages in his philosophical writing, Professor Whitehead has put this conclusion on a sound metaphysical basis, so that it is more than a mere opinion. "Advance or Decadence," he says, "are the only choices offered to mankind.

The pure conservative is fighting against the essence of the universe."[2]

Whatever else may be the character of the redemptive society which the crisis of our time demands, it is at least clear that the society must make the habit of adventure central to its life. If this were done, vast changes might come quickly. Just as Wesley's class meetings were markedly different from what had been seen before in the religious life of England, so we may need to produce fellowships markedly different from what has been seen before in the religious life of America. It may be that the church of tomorrow will be as different from the church of today as a modern transport plane is different from the little machine the Wright brothers flew at Kittyhawk. It should not be forgotten that the Christian religion began as such an adventure in fellowship, the members often meeting in synagogues, but introducing real novelty into the association as their needs became clear. One important innovation was the regular communal meal, with the use of ordinary food. It would not be false to say that their central room was a dining room. It is conceivable that ours should be the same. In any case, those who break bread together have a basis of genuine fellowship and the sad fact is that this is what so many organizations now lack. The plan of the chapel, which will be the dominant feature of the Kirkridge Community in the Pennsylvania mountains, is that of a building constructed entirely about a huge, centrally located and rough-hewn communion table.

We must rid our minds of most current conceptions about

[2] *Adventures of Ideas*, p. 354.

what a church should be in order to try to see what the real needs of men are. Perhaps there ought not to be any distinction at all between clergy and laity; perhaps the life of the church should function better without the ownership of buildings or any property. Many of the early Christian groups met in homes and several met in caves, while some of the seventeenth-century Quaker meetings were held in prison. Perhaps real membership should be rigorously restricted to the deeply convinced; perhaps the normal unit should be the small cell rather than the large gathering. Many churches would be ten times as influential if their membership were half as great.

This list of suggestions could be enlarged. It *will* be enlarged by any group of people who try to put into this question the same bold thinking that our best scientists have already put into the questions which they have been so extraordinarily successful in answering, and the same disciplined imagination that our best architects have put into new buildings. We do not know what the church of the future ought to be, but we can be reasonably sure that it ought to be very different from the church as we know it today. "If something radical is to happen to society," says Dr. Oldham, "something radical must happen to the church." We are due for great changes and we must not resist them. Far from that, we must help to produce them.

It is good to see the evidence that Christians are already at this task of creative dreaming on the question of what a truly redemptive fellowship might be. New movements have been started already, both within the churches and outside them. For the most part, however, the people in these movements are separated from those in other and similar movements, with little sense of sharing in a world-wide enterprise. Some are lonely thinkers, almost unaware that others have had their same impatience with what is offered and the same high vision of what might be accomplished. Others are unaware of similar experiments which have occurred in the past, experiments from which they might learn in planning their contemporary efforts. Success will not come except as we help each other.

It is instructive to note that many of the most encouraging experiments in the past have been, not new churches, but new orders within the Church. It has been part of the genius of the Roman Catholic church to include new life, within the general framework of the church, by the formation of various orders. The well-known ones, such as the Dominican, the Franciscan and the Jesuit, have differed markedly from one another, but all have essentially the same relationship to the church as a whole in that they are orders within it. This helps them to make a *reformation within* rather than a *reformation from*. There seems to be no good reason why an adventurous Christianity might not follow this same policy outside the Catholic body. This has already been done, in part, in the formation of several societies such as Christian Endeavor, the Y.W.C.A., the Student Volunteer movement, the Intervarsity Christian Fellowship and many more. All of these are horizontal in that they cut across all denominational lines and seek to make their members *loyal to* their churches rather than *divided from* their churches. All seek, in some sense or other, to be orders within the Church Universal. It is unfortunate that some societies which begin with this high conception end dismally by becoming sects.

One of the most encouraging aspects of our time is that there is already a stirring of the imagination with the introduction of orders or quasi orders. Some involve dangerous tendencies and each may be inadequate, but this is the way new life comes. Most really vital movements seem dangerous and queer when they begin. The early Christians did not always commend themselves to their neighbors, partly because they included, as any vigorous movement does, some of the lunatic fringe. Francis of Assisi and the radical men about him certainly constituted a thorn in the flesh for their respectable neighbors. It is one of the merits of Bernard Shaw's play, *St. Joan,* that he has reminded us how difficult it is to have live saints as associates, and how much more comfortable it is to revere them long after they are dead. Present-day Quakers are highly honored all over the world, regardless of differences of faith, but it was not always so. Some of the seventeenth-century Quakers were so obstreperous that we can understand why they were persecuted and even hanged, though we cannot condone the persecution. It was likewise a sin to burn Servetus, but it is obvious that he asked for it. Modern Methodists are highly respectable citizens, but in the eighteenth century even Bishop Butler considered John Wesley a dangerous radical.

In view of this experience we must not look for perfection in new orders, but rather for vigor and adventure, in the hope that wisdom may come—and come without destroying the vigor. Among the most interesting of new societies which involve something of the character of orders within the Church Universal are Alcoholics Anonymous, the League of the Kingdom, the New Life Movement and the Wider Quaker Fellowship. Common to many of these is the idea that life is best fostered by the formation of small cells, each with a life of its own, which can unite to form larger bodies as the cells of the physical body unite. Growth comes, all agree, by cell division.

On a different level we find a movement like that centering in the island of Iona, uniting physical work, meditation, study and discipline and dedicated to the task of "the conversion of Scotland." The closest approximation to such fellowship in America has been found in the work camps, especially those fostered by the American Friends Service Committee.

On a third level are found what are usually called cults, among them the movements associated with Father Divine and Jehovah's Witnesses. These and many more are growing rapidly, partly because they demand so much more of their members than does the average respectable church. These associations tend to become intense fellowships, in which membership is taken seriously and whose members feel a marked responsibility for the total welfare of one another. Though the ideas of these movements may be far from the ideas of primitive Christianity, they come closer to primitive Christianity in their intense commitment of their total lives than do most other groups of people in the modern world.

Living in a time which provides us with so much relevant contemporary experience, as well as the experience of former generations, we should be able to employ a disciplined imagination to good advantage in determining what the essential features of a truly redemptive society may be. We live in what seems to be a time of unusual ferment and it is good to be part of this intellectual agitation.

Though Catholicism and Protestantism provide the two chief alternatives for modern man, we dare not be satisfied with either of them in the form in which they now normally appear. In one sense we must go beyond both of them and in another sense we must go behind both of them. Fortunately, the two directions are not incompatible. In going beyond them to what ought to be we may, at the same time, be going behind them to that from which both have departed.

In our recognition that we must go beyond both Catholicism and Protestantism we are helped by the experience of the early Quaker societies, which proposed to themselves exactly this aim. George Fox, William Penn, Robert Barclay and others who shared the remarkable fellowship that arose first out of the dark years of the Cromwellian period were convinced that the way to go beyond both Catholics and Protestants was to pierce all artificiality and recover radical Christianity. This root Christianity inherent in all forms, but often obscured by them, would be similar to that experienced by the simple fellowships of the first century of our era. Thus a characteristic book title, among those produced by William Penn, was *Primitive Christianity Revived*. It cannot be too clearly stated that what early Friends intended was a truly *radical* experiment. George Fox proposed to cut straight through all the religious red tape. If anything seemed artificial and unnecessary, the young shoemaker's apprentice determined to dispense with it, no matter how precious it might have been at other times or how glorified by tradition. Naked reality was what he sought. It is to this that William James was referring when he said, "The Quaker religion is something which it is impossible to overpraise. In a day of shams, it was a religion of veracity rooted in spiritual inwardness and a return to something more like the original gospel truth than men had ever known in England."

George Fox was not a learned man. He knew very little about Christian history between the first and the seventeenth centuries but he did know the difference between essentials and nonessentials. Consequently he paid no real attention either to sacraments and liturgical forms made impressive by long usage or to a priesthood claiming apostolic authority by a succession secured through episcopal ordination. Much as Dr. Johnson later "refuted" Bishop Berkeley by kicking a stone, Fox refuted the sacerdotalists by the direct appeal to experience. He *saw* unordained men, and even women, ministering with apostolic power. What other evidence could be required?

Though Fox did not claim to know the fine points of the theory of ordination and apostolic succession, he did know that men might be perfectly regular on these points and yet grossly lacking in the evidence either of love of the brethren or of closeness to God. He was aware that men might cling to these externals of the faith when the life had departed from them. He saw that men could easily be meticulous about these matters or even about dogmatic formulations of faith and yet be careless about the weightier matters of mercy, justice and truth. What did he care about the external credentials of the "true Church" when he knew in his own soul the kind of illumination that placed him in the order of prophets and apostles? What he proposed, quite simply, was an experiment in veracity.

The experiment has been useful chiefly because it has constituted a direct and open challenge to dogmatic exclusiveness, wherever found. Through three centuries, Friends have been a problem to the creed makers. Here are people who give considerable evidence that they are Christians, but they break the neatly stated rules. How can you define Christians as baptized persons when some whose Christianity is everywhere recognized have never been baptized, at least not in the sense intended? *Thus experience, produced by experiment, checks dogma. This truly is scientific method.*

There is in the world today a great deal of fruitless argument, especially between Protestants and Roman Catholics, over the question what the true Church is and who is in it. The Quaker experiment cuts straight across this argument by the application of the experimental test. Do you want to know whether a group is part of the true Church? Very well, note whether they love each other; note whether their hearts are quickened by the love of the living God; note whether they show that they have the mind of Christ in them. No other credentials are needed. If these are lacking, all reference to historical origin and development is meaningless anyway. Ask, of any group, not how it got here but where it is now. The golden text of all this emphasis on radical veracity is found in a memorable sentence from the pen of Robert Barclay, who, like Fox, was impatient of artificiality. "It is the life of Christianity taking place in the heart that makes a Christian; and so it is a number of such being alive, joined together in the life of Christianity, that makes a Church of Christ; and it is all those that are thus alive and quickened, considered together, that make the Catholic Church of Christ."[3] Such a sentence suggests nothing to be added or taken away. Anyone can use this test

[3] *Apology,* 10.

now, for it belongs to all. It is one of the best fruits of the experiment.

The chief value of an experiment is that we can learn from it, both in its successes and in its failures. The Quaker experiment can teach something to all adventurers in that it shows (1) how it is possible to keep a sense of direct immediacy without the sterility of isolated individualism and likewise (2) how to combine the advantage of a living ministry with the advantages of lay religion by taking seriously the doctrine of the priesthood of the believer. Furthermore it shows (3) how to combine the deep reverence of quiet worship with intense activity in social reconstruction that is best expressed by the sacred word "concern." On the other hand, the Quaker experiment involves many failures which should serve us as warnings. The chief failure has lain in the willingness to become one denomination among others, instead of a continuous ferment among all.

This brief analysis of one historic experiment suggests to us a way in which we can learn from many. If we are ecumenical Christians, all such experience, from whatever quarter, is relevant to our undertaking. We cannot be loyal to adventurous movements in the past by copying precisely from their procedure; the only way in which we can be loyal to an adventurous movement is by going beyond it in being adventurous ourselves. The essential experiment we need to make in our day is an experiment in radical Christianity. *The redemptive society we need is an order within the Church Universal, devoted to the recovery and fulfillment of radical Christianity.* In the following chapters we shall seek to outline some of the relevant features which must be included in the formation of such societies.

Chapter III

THE FELLOWSHIP OF THE CONCERNED

Civilization develops only where considerable numbers of men work together for common ends.

—GEORGE FOOT MOORE

If the argument of the preceding chapter is valid we need to engage seriously in the enterprise of creative dreaming concerning what the nature of a redemptive society, fitted to the needs of our crucial time, might be. Very well, let us dream! Is there some better way than those we now know in which men and women may be bound together for redemptive purposes at this juncture of history? As we try to answer this question we must always realize that, in practice, ideal possibilities cannot be given complete embodiment. But that need not deter us. We are glad it did not deter Plato in his dreaming of the *Republic* or Augustine in dreaming of the *City of God*. Even though we do not achieve all that the time requires, we may achieve more than if we refused to try. As was intimated in the preceding chapter, Columbus would not have found America if he had not sought the coast of China. Though the perfect embodiment

58

of the dream is never expected, it is wise to do our dreaming on the basis of actuality. What do we have already, in fact, on which a more ideal order could be built? The answer here is fortunately clear. We have the horizontal fellowship which cuts across all boundaries. There are in the world today thousands of men and women who already accept the same essential gospel, use the same language and make some effort to live and work in the same way. They are vastly closer to one another than they are to their supposed fellow members in their own organizations. This new existential fellowship crosses boundaries which, in theory, cannot be crossed. For example, I am closer, in fundamental sympathies and convictions, to some Catholic priests than I am to some of my fellow Quakers. At the same time I am closer to some who are wholly outside any church affiliation than I am to thousands of alleged church members. I believe that many readers will report similar experiences.

Here, then, is a realistic basis of advance. The order we seek is already in being and requires only development to become truly powerful. Starting with this sober realism we can use our minds to sharpen the lines, produce an acceptable discipline, and help people to be conscious of the possibilities inherent in the fellowship they already have. What is required is not organization, in the sense of the election of officers or the establishment of headquarters; what is required is organization in the radically different sense of a common understanding of purposes and the inauguration of joint means of accomplishing them. The horizontal alignment will be strengthened if its members take membership seriously and have some general agreement in detail concerning what membership involves. It must always be modest and unostentatious, as was the original Franciscan order, where all were Friars Minor in order that none might be Friar Major. It would ruin the new order if it were to promote an international congress and present a spectacle. Then there would be elections, resolutions and committees, and decay would already be well advanced. Our hope lies, rather, in the conscious existence and growth of a relatively unorganized order, preferably an order without a name, yet one in which the members would recognize one another by the level of their concern. Nameless in practice, it would, in reality, be the Order of the Concerned.

Such an order might become a leavening influence in all the churches and in our total civilization. Chapters are already in being in some parts of our country and a few of these are beginning to realize how truly universal is the spontaneous movement to which they actually, though not nominally, belong. There are many who refuse to join the church as they know it because it is so tame or so worldly and self-seeking, but they might join a fellowship which escapes tameness by the recovery of the lost urgency of the Christian faith, and which escapes worldliness by the fact that it wholly renounces ostentation and display. Why should not such concerned groups, in all churches and outside all churches, be as effective in the reconstruction of our total life as the disciplined groups which constitute the communist cells now are in the spread of their particular gospel?

The chief reason why the church as we now know it is not more effective than it is, is the fact that membership has become almost meaningless. Once "member" was a glorious word, signifying a real interpenetration of lives for a noble purpose, but now the figure of speech has worn smooth. Membership is now largely *paper* membership. Members have their names on books because once they were accepted and there has been no sufficient reason since then to delete their names. Meanwhile they may absent themselves wholly from public worship, they may take no part in the making of group decisions, they may give no money and they may do absolutely nothing to spread the gospel. The membership of such a person is clearly a fiction. If we seek renewal of life one way of advance lies in the direction of *veracity in membership.* Let us begin, therefore, by outlining the minimum conditions of membership in the new order which is coming into being so rapidly and to which some of us aspire to belong.

The minimum conditions of membership in the nameless order of the Church Universal are five: *commitment, witness, fellowship, vocation* and *discipline.* Since these are not self-explanatory, each demands some amplification at this point.

1. By commitment is meant the acceptance of convictions, not merely by intellectual assent, but by a full act of the will. The fundamental insight of Blaise Pascal, that faith is not supine acceptance of dogma, but rather something in the nature of a gamble, has been accepted by almost all subsequent thinkers. Religion, as many of us understand it, is not the acceptance of conventional standards of behavior and it is not primarily an effort to save our own puny souls; *it is the exciting venture of faith in which we bet that God really is, that this is His world, and that He is like Jesus Christ.*

It is the essence of a gamble that the gambler either wins or loses; he is either right or wrong. There is no middle ground. So it is with our supreme gamble. Our faith is either true to reality or it is a horrible delusion. If it is not true, it is an evil.

Commitment means willingness to take the plunge, to run the risk of seeming ridiculous if we turn out to be wrong. It is, of course, not a *wild* leap, since there is so much of a wholly intellectual nature to support our position, but, in the end, it is always a leap. We cannot remain forever on the springboard poised for the leap. To refuse to decide is itself one decision and essentially a negative decision.

Here, then, is the first plank in our platform. We seek groups of genuinely committed men and women, men and women who continue to be perplexed and doubtful in many areas of their experience but who are willing to follow one major clue wherever it may lead. Such people will believe that God has a purpose for the world, so that there is potential meaning in history. Their greatest desire is to learn that purpose and to carry it forward. People who understand their religion as absolute commitment to what is recognized as absolutely worthy cannot fail to recognize their need of help in knowing what is absolutely worthy. There have been such various objects of supreme loyalty; how are we to choose between them? Increasingly, through the centuries, we have found in the life, teachings and death of Jesus Christ a convincing answer. He, of all, inspires our full confidence. A Christian is one who will stake everything on this confidence. We do not know all the answers, and we are very sure that there is more truth still waiting to break forth, but we are willing to risk our present and eternal destiny on the conviction that the light seen in the face of Jesus Christ is the surest light we can know. We crucified Him on a stick, says Shaw, but we have always had a curious feeling that He somehow "managed to get hold of the right end of it."[1]

Those with this central conviction still cannot see the whole way in any problem and they know that answers to ultimate problems are seldom simple or easy, but they believe that the light will go with them as they walk. Obedience, they agree, is the organ of knowledge, while courage to follow the light already seen is the precondition of the emergence of more light. Thus their religion, instead of being the dull and lifeless thing which so many honest pagans rightly detest, may be a constant adventure.

The mood of commitment may be realized in many different aspects of our lives and may become a way of approaching all greatness. In art, for example, only the committed grasp the true glory of beauty. The clearest illustration of this principle is found in marriage. The deepest joys of marriage are not experienced by those who keep their fingers crossed, ready to dissolve the "contract" if it fails, but by those who commit themselves without reservations, *for better and for worse*. For such, the relation goes beyond the status of contract to that of sacrament, and this, as millions have learned, is the path of glory.

It cannot be too strongly pointed out that such commitment involves a deep humility. There is always, in our sinful world, the danger of self-righteousness or spiritual pride, but a full acceptance of the experience of commitment helps mightily to avoid this pride. The committed Christian does not claim to have arrived; he is, instead, willing to start. He is, accordingly, perplexed, but not unto despair. He knows that at best we touch only the fringe of the divine

[1] Preface to *Androcles and the Lion*, p. 1.

garment and that even the little we see is seen through a glass darkly, but he is unwilling, for that reason, to fall back into skeptical futility. He has seen a tiny light and that light he will follow, even though he does not know all the answers.

Those who make up the nameless order are not united by their virtue, for they are not virtuous; neither are they united by their superior intelligence or piety. Their only bond of union is their *concern*. This is the early Christian pattern, according to which we learn that "not many wise men . . . , not many mighty, not many noble"[2] were called. In spite of all its failures the Church of Jesus Christ has kept much of this spirit to this day, so that, in contrast to secular societies, a sense of unworthiness is the prime condition of entrance. Nobody has said this better, in recent times, than has Charles Clayton Morrison in his justly famous Beecher Lectures: "The Christian church is not a society of integrated personalities, nor of philosophers, nor of mystics, nor even of good people. It is a society of broken personalities, of men and women with troubled minds, of people who know that they are not good. The Christian church is a society of sinners. It is the only society in the world, membership in which is based upon the single qualification that the candidate shall be unworthy of membership."[3]

2. That *witness* should be the second plank in the platform of the new order follows directly from attention to the New Testament model. In the Sermon on the Mount, the reference to the light of the world follows immediately

[2] I Corinthians 1:26.
[3] Charles Clayton Morrison, *What Is Christianity?* Willett, Clark and Company, 1940, p. 211.

the reference to the salt of the earth. If it is the whole company of committed souls who are the salt of the earth, it follows that they must be unapologetic in making their witness before the world, which is in such constant danger of decay. The ancient words have been a source of embarrassment to modern lukewarm Christians who, like their neighbors, are horribly afraid of "sticking their necks out." It is highly unfashionable to take an unapologetic position and let others know where we stand; it seems so immodest. Yet here are the embarrassing words: "Ye are the light of the world. A city that is set on an hill cannot be hid. Neither do men light a candle, and put it under a bushel, but on a candlestick; and it giveth light unto all that are in the house. Let your light so shine before men, that they may see your good works, and glorify your Father which is in heaven."[4]

Our normal reaction to these unequivocal words of our Master provides an interesting illustration of how easy self-delusion is. Our self-delusion in this case consists in the interpretation of our moral failure as a positive virtue. Being unwilling to stand up and be counted, we call this humility, when it is really cowardice. We quote, in self-defense, another sentence of Jesus about not occupying the front seats in the synagogue. But all this is patently false, since the temptation to occupy the front seats of the synagogue is not the temptation of our time, whatever it may once have been. The temptation now is to occupy the rear seats in the synagogue, to avoid responsibility, to play the easy and comfortable role of spectator. It is much easier to be a spectator, for the spectator seldom seems ridiculous. If you never go out on a limb, it will never be cut off while you are sitting on

[4] Matthew 5:14-16.

it. All this is the cowardly and fashionable philosophy of our day. It is the philosophy of a tired people and its ultimate goal is complete futility.

There is no doubt that all the powerful periods of Christian history have been marked by the acceptance of witness. The friar, by donning his habit, told the world where he stood. The young and gay Elizabeth Fry, when she put on the sober Quaker bonnet and shawl, was standing up to be counted, burdensome as that experience might be. The humble member of the Methodist class meeting arose among his fellows and, no matter how halting the words, tried to tell of his love for his Saviour and thereby announce which side he was on. That all this can be done in a way wholly consistent with personal humility is abundantly clear. The person who makes such a witness is announcing, not his own goodness, but the love of God and his personal willingness to serve under that banner.

One of the most revealing marks of our current Christianity at the middle of the twentieth century is the relative absence of public witness to the faith. Even the Methodists have lost it; their class meetings having fallen into decay and their testimony meetings, where still extant, having become gatherings confined chiefly to old ladies. Meanwhile the "members" leave it all to the clergyman. Isn't that what he is hired for? He is professionally religious, so it is right that he should speak and offer vocal prayer, but that is not for laymen. All this means decline. It is on a level with our commercial sports in which the multitude watch and the experts perform.

One of the simplest ways in which an ordinary church could begin to become an Order of the Concerned would be for the clergy to encourage the participation of the laity in the conduct of public worship. Most of the churches have permissive rubrics, but they do nothing about this, partly because it is easier to stay in the same old rut. The great advantage which accrues when a lay member reads the Scripture or offers vocal prayer is that this becomes his means of public witness. It may not do the others good, but it does him good. The most fortunate single feature of preaching is the beneficent effect on the one who does the preaching. Witness strengthens his Christian commitment because he has taken a public stand before his fellows. That the lay-men know very well that this is what it means is shown by the manner in which some refuse to participate when invited. They are afraid to make a public witness because more will be expected of them by their neighbors, once they make such a witness.

The fashionable religion of our day is deeply apologetic. Most people hesitate to be known as atheists, but they hesi-tate, almost equally, to be known as convinced Christians. That is bad form; it approaches the fanatical; it is like getting hot and bothered. The mood of relative detachment is far more comfortable because it involves so few demands. Mil-lions in our generation are more afraid of seeming pious than they are of seeming wicked, and to make a public wit-ness is to run the risk of seeming to think oneself better than one's neighbors. Most of us have grown up with the supposition that hypocrisy means trying to hide our sin by appearing better than we are. Today, however, all this is reversed. The conventional pose now is that of the inverted hypocrisy in which we try to hide our virtue and seem worse than we are. Most of the writers in support of large-scale allocation of American funds for the reconstruction of Europe go out of their way to dissociate themselves from the suggestion that this ought to be done on moral grounds or for the sake of the people. Altruism, we gather, is something that no self-respecting person would be caught committing. We are assured, in the strongest language, that the proposed action is thoroughly regular because it is purely in our national self-interest.

Whatever the mood of this time, it is perfectly clear that our hope lies in the acceptance of an unapologetic faith. For some, at least, the decision to stand unapologetically for the gospel has been tantamount to a new conversion. It brings peace; it dissolves fears; it snaps fingers at ridicule. Herein lies much of the power of many of the new cults, which demand public witness as a first evidence of sincerity, and whose members are so often placed in positions where they are immediately subjected to ridicule. Any group that is wholly unapologetic will work wonders in any community. Ten such will accomplish more in any Sodom[5] than will a thousand lukewarm "members." What we seek, then, is the Fellowship of the Unashamed. They will know one another by their faces, for they will be unabashed. They will have one golden text, and that text will be the sixteenth verse of the first chapter of Romans.

3. Unless it involves *fellowship* that is deep and inclusive, church membership is always nominal rather than real. Without genuine fellowship there is no *koinonia*. There are, indeed, times in our lives when we wish to enter a darkened church, pray and leave without speaking to another human being, but such religious experience is not satisfactory as a

[5] Genesis 18:32.

steady diet. The normal religious experience is that in which the society of worship becomes also a society of friends. We must be *disciples,* we must be *catholics,* but, above all, we must be *brethren.* Inner illumination alone, important as it is, may produce the self-centered and the bizarre, with no outside checks on either ideas or conduct. The sense of urgency alone may produce unbalanced fanaticism, but men and women who submit to the disciplines of fellowship, seeking group guidance in major decisions and recognizing the authority of group experience, are largely saved from these extravagances. The lesson of many religious societies is that, while individual mysticism may be dangrous, group mysticism tends to be wholly beneficent.

The heart of the idea of membership as experienced by the early Christian fellowship, and as interpreted to the society at Corinth, was that of being members one of another. They, like other groups in which there has been a serious attempt to practice radical Christianity, found that membership in the Body of Christ causes men and women to temper their own wishes by the wishes and needs of their fellow members. The early Christian society at Jerusalem believed that the new life into which they had entered involved not only the sharing of prayers but the sharing of food and all material possessions. The result, we are told, was gladness and singleness of heart.[6]

The pattern of the early Jerusalem society has inspired a succession of experiments through the centuries, though most of them have failed. One shining example of continued success, though in a modest way, is that of the Bruderhof, which has existed, often with severe persecution, for four hundred years. Recently Bruderhof colonies have been estab-

[6] Acts 2:46.

lished in England, Canada and Paraguay. The essence of the Bruderhof idea is the acceptance of responsibility for one's fellows and the children of one's fellows. It is an effort to extend the spirit of the family to the entire community. This is clearly a dangerous idea, fraught with many difficulties and feasible only at a high level of devotion. "It is important," writes a member from Paraguay, "that the fellowship of the group be so strong that the members can truly practise *an unlimited liability for each other.*"

Noble as the Bruderhof idea is, and valuable as it may be when embodied in an actual community, it seems clear that most of us must find some other way. It is the ordinary lump of ordinary life that must be leavened, and there is where our major responsibility lies. Our question is how, in the midst of ordinary existence, as housewives and merchants and teachers and nurses and parents, we can illustrate the maximum fellowship which such existence allows. What we can be sure is that there are many fruitful possibilities which we have not yet considered.

One of the most valuable discoveries or rediscoveries of our time, in regard to evangelism, is that of the house party. Why, some began to ask almost a generation ago, could not this hitherto secular social institution be employed for the Kingdom of God? Among those who have used the method most successfully are the members of the Oxford Groups. These people made the crucial mistake of introducing the element of social snobbery into the house-party idea, but this is not inherent in it and ought not to deter us from using the method in a wholly modest and democratic way. It is now being so used by Stanley Jones and many more. In Britain there is a successful variant of the system in the institution of "week-end settlements," usually held at some modest country inn and limited in attendance to twenty or twenty-five persons.

What we learn from such experience is that the house party makes possible an intensity of fellowship greater than that of an ordinary conference, with its numbers and its public meetings, and vastly greater than that of an ordinary church, where people may sit on the same benches one hour a week for years and never really *know* one another. It is not uncommon for a student to feel that he has gained more, in the development of moral purpose, from a single intense week end, than from years in college. The reason for this is that lives join *organically* in the intense fellowship, whereas usually lives touch only as do marbles in a bag. Because of the ease of modern transportation, it should be possible to multiply enormously the number of such creative fellowships in which, for at least forty-eight hours, people dine together, wash dishes together, pray together, sit silent together and talk together. Why should not many local church buildings, especially in quiet country places, be made into such settlements? Usually there is already a kitchen, as well as a dining room, and it is a simple matter to put up cots for sleeping. Again, the prime requirement is imagination.

For those who cannot attend such specialized fellowships, there is always that sacred institution, the church supper. We smile, sometimes, at the church supper, but we are not wise when we do so. *It is the oldest Christian ritual.* It is one spontaneous way of expressing the reality of *koinonia.* In hundreds of parishes it is actually a more valuable experience than is the Sunday morning hour of worship. If we were truly wise we should build on this sound base rather than despise it, for the church supper can become the love feast. Once a week it is possible to stand in the tradition of the church at Jerusalem and "continuing steadfastly in the apostles' doctrine and fellowship, in breaking bread, and in prayers, have all things in common." This is part of that Christian communism which makes doctrinaire communism seem shabby by comparison. It should include all ages and all races, because we are all children of a common Father.

Recently several churches with large nominal membership have experienced a new burst of life by dividing all members into zones. One strong church of two thousand persons now has twenty-eight zones with weekly meetings in homes in each zone. Here is the resurrection of "the church that is in thine house." These meetings are times of deep fellowship, where those who have long been neighbors geographically become neighbors in fact, but this fellowship is based on something more profound than secular sociability. The groups hold together because of serious study of the same book, because of quiet worship and because of devoted labor on the part of group conveners.

A further practical step in the promotion of fellowship, which a few have undertaken, is the application in common life of the Bruderhof concept of *unlimited liability* for one another. If a redemptive society has reality, the members will not allow one single member to struggle alone with a fianancial difficulty. Often a family with young children must be helped, especially in the case of catastrophic illness which ordinary hospital insurance does not cover. If a member dies without insurance, his children must not be left in want. We tend to follow this line of action in severe situations, but we miss it in situations less severe; yet it is in the less severe situations that most of us can be efficacious. Why, for instance, should not the older women of a redemptive fellowship organize themselves to serve without pay in relieving the younger parents who cannot afford to hire people to sit in their homes while they go out either for pleasure or for service? This would be very easy to do but it almost never occurs. Unless we are faithful in the little, as regards an intensive fellowship, we are not likely to be faithful in the large.

4. The fourth minimum criterion of membership in a new order is the acceptance of *vocation*. This is a magnificent idea and requires some explanation. It means that all true members must be fountains, not cisterns. It means that each member must be willing to think of himself as engaged in the ministry, by a divine imperative. If "member" is to regain positive significance in our vocabulary, we must think of all recruits as entering a new estate, beyond clergy and beyond laity. In the new order there are no clergymen and no laymen, but all are engaged in the same divine vocation, which means putting the claims of the Kingdom of God first, no matter what profession one may follow. *The formula is that vocation has priority over profession.*

In nearly all the examples we have mentioned, in which there has been a burst of new Christian life, this criterion has been observed. In the beginning of the Christian cause all were ministers. *Member* equaled *evangelist* equaled *missionary*. There was no place within the society for the observer, the mere supporter or the nominal member. This is the conclusion of Auguste Sabatier, on the basis of his monumental study of early Christianity, and as expressed in his definitive work of scholarship. "At this period," he says, "we find no trace of a division of Christians into clergy and laity. All formed the elect people, and conversely, this people was collectively a people of priests and prophets. There were no passive members. The most humble had their share of activity and were by no means least necessary."[7] St. Paul mentions those who had *ordained themselves*[8] to the service of the community, while "apostle" meant nothing but missionary. We find, in the beginning, no formal institution of episcopacy and no hierarchy whatsoever. On this point, says Sabatier, "the testimony of the early Church is universal, and admits of not a single exception."[9]

The greatest single strength of the seventeenth-century Quaker movement is that it involved only active workers. A similar practice is followed by Jehovah's Witnesses and various other virile groups of our day. All the evidence shows that any society, anywhere, which will adopt this practice will be dynamic in any culture. If we want to make a difference, here is a clear way. *Make all, within your society, members of the crew and permit no passengers.* Since the children of darkness are often wiser, in their day, than are the children of light, Adolf Hitler accepted this principle unequivocally in his organization of the party and expressed it clearly in *Mein Kampf.*

There was a time when, especially in evangelical circles, much was made of a call to the ministry. A standard feature of revivals was the attention paid, not only to new converts to the faith, but also to those who felt and accepted a call to "full-time Christian service." This was a valid and worth-

[7] Auguste Sabatier, *Religions of Authority and the Religion of the Spirit,* Hodder and Stoughton, 1904, pp. 71, 72.
[8] I Corinthians 16:15.
[9] *Op. cit.,* p. 77.

while procedure, but it did not go far enough. By full-time Christian service was meant the life of the pastor, missionary, deaconess, etc. But why stop there? If this is God's world, all of it, and if all Christians are called, as the New Testament declares, to a royal priesthood, why should the sense of vocation be thus arbitrarily limited? Why cannot a man be called to be a Christian chemist, why cannot a woman be called to be a Christian homekeeper or nurse? If we were to take the gospel seriously this is exactly the way it would be.

If we accept the proposition that *member = evangelist = missionary* we begin to understand what the true relation between vocation and profession really is. Most of us must have professions, both because the world needs work done and because we need to earn a living for ourselves and our families, but the convinced Christian will choose both his profession and his place and manner of conducting it in the light of a prior loyalty. A Christian doctor will not choose his location wholly in the light of potential income and professional advancement or prestige but in the light of his service to the Christian cause. A Christian doctor is not one who goes to the foreign field but one, anywhere, who places vocation above profession.

Though there is no possibility of hierarchy in a society which seeks to be radically Christian, there can be a division of labor. One possible task is that of pastor, since the care which a good pastor provides is one of the most needed of services. It is a noble thing to be a Christian pastor, nourishing the common life and curing sick souls, but it is no more a holy task than that of the Christian banker. The modern world, of course, does not accept this. In the modern world, we confuse the notion of being professionally pastoral with the notion of being professionally religious. We think the clergyman is professionally religious and we treat him so. We ask him to say grace at service club luncheons and we ask him to offer invocations at high school commencements. We moderate our speech when we find that "a man of the cloth" is in the party. This widespread notion of a "man of the cloth," a variant of the primitive notion of "medicine man," is wholly pernicious. By making religion a profession rather than a vocation, the ordinary member is relieved of a sense of urgent responsibility and becomes a spectator when he ought to be a participator.

Most people in the world will not be, and ought not to be, pastors. Can we give the majority some guidance in the particular decisions they are to make in the light of the revolutionary notion of vocation? Perhaps the greatest help we can give, especially to young people, lies in the depiction of concrete tasks needed mightily in our day. Though there are many of these, five can be stressed at this point. These are five possible classifications within the nameless fellowship.

a. *The first need is for colonists.* This is the largest single classification of "real members" and can include almost any serious person. We need a number of men and women who will consider seriously their place of abode and their professional work in the light of the way in which they can foster the growth of redemptive fellowships. Sometimes several families should colonize together as was so frequently done in the early days. Nearly all those early American rural communities which produced a level of life far out of proportion to neighboring communities were established in this way. Striking examples, out of many, are Salem, Indiana, and Grinnell, Iowa. Such places were colonized by the conscious association of deeply concerned families. The point is that this can happen again and keep on happening, if only we exercise some imagination in the conduct of our lives and do not follow the path of least resistance.

Though colonization in the country is most immediately appealing, we must realize that for many this would be an escape and therefore evil. Most people now live in cities and this is where most vocational Christians should colonize. We must not forget that, after the close of the Galilean ministry, the Christian societies which did so much to turn the world upside down were located in large cities. Its first centers were Antioch, Tarsus, Ephesus, Smyrna, Philippi, Corinth, Alexandria, Rome.

What we must do is to select our place of labor on the basis of recognized need and opportunity. Go where you can make the largest contribution before you die. Find the fellowship which your presence will strengthen or find a town where you may start one by the dint of long-continued effort in one place. This conception can especially dignify the Christian vocation of women, since women are colonists par excellence. The profession of homekeeper, perhaps the noblest in the world, and the one that *should* be termed sacred if any is, lends itself to the establishment of centers of Christian influence. In home after home St. Paul found a base of operations. Together such homes can form a strong chain.

b. *The second need in vocational membership is for itinerants.* The little Christian communities, which we have taken as our ancient models, were the work of itinerant missionaries. This work can often be carried on, as St. Paul demonstrated, in conjunction with some other occupation, by which a living is earned and useful contacts are made. Many men and women who believe that they have a flair for the itinerant ministry, bringing new life into many isolated fellowships, may choose their professional work in the light of this task. For example, there is one highly successful itinerant in America who has deliberately accepted, in his industry, the task of traveling salesman because this makes it possible for his itinerant vocation to be realized. He tries to plan his business trips in the light of his service to the Kingdom of God. It is clear that this practice could be followed in many kinds of remunerative and useful work. Our failure lies, not in the difficulty of the combination, but in the fact that such considerations are so seldom even considered in our major decisions.

c. *A third demand is for Christian politicians.* There are a few men and women in politics because of a high sense of responsibility, but not nearly enough. For the most part, the people of deep moral convictions are so revolted by the corruption and deceit seemingly inherent in the political game that they wash their hands of it. But this is a grievous mistake, since it merely gives the unscrupulous an uncontended field. If we care about our total culture, which we must, we shall try to produce, within our order, a guild of Christian politicians determined to try to make their influence felt, no matter how long and discouraging the road may be. A small group in Congress, meeting regularly as the Fellowship of the Concerned and seeking group guidance in important decisions, might be far more influential than we can now imagine. In any case, the state is part of the world which needs to be redeemed.

d. *A fourth classification is that of Christian scholars.* We have many young people who propose to enter a life of scholarship, usually with an eye to university teaching, but they are frequently very lonely. If they could think of themselves, in all humility, as members of a guild of Christian thinkers, they would be strengthened in the pagan atmosphere into which they are so often thrown and to which so many succumb. It is well known that numbers of our universities, including those founded originally by the sacrifice and devotion of Christian people, are almost wholly secular or pagan. In some of them a philosophic naturalism has come to be an almost rigid orthodoxy. The problem of the Christian scholar in this situation is parallel to that of the Christian politician in Congress.

In our fields of Christian scholarship all subjects of human interest must be included. Any notion that this classification is only for those teaching Bible, religion or philosophy would be wholly damaging. In many universities the appointments in chemistry or in history are far more important, in the light of a redemptive society, than is an appointment in Biblical literature. It is assumed in advance that the professor of Bible is devout; that is part of his job and his position is accordingly discounted. But the world does not suppose that it is part of the job of the professor of physics to be a member of a redemptive society. We are shocked if he is, but the shock is highly beneficent.

It is good to know that the idea of Christian professor is growing and that several associations devoted to this idea have been formed. This is important for our total civilization because universities and colleges are our vanguard; they lead the way. We need to pioneer again in the formation of

Christian colleges and in the reformation of those which we have begun to lose. In this it will be important to accept the premise that a Christian college is not one which, somewhere in its curriculum, offers a course in Biblical literature or comparative religions, but rather one which seeks to instill Christian convictions into all phases of college experience, both intellectual and practical.

e. *A fifth and final classification, in this tentative list, is that of writer.* This must be included because the written word is still efficacious in our modern life. We need gifted and disciplined minds, willing to use their powers to spread the gospel and thus reach millions who can never be reached by the spoken word because they are not present where it is spoken. A brilliant example of how well this can be done is provided by the career of C. S. Lewis. This able writer has had a remarkable influence in a series of small books, the size of which has been chosen deliberately in order to encourage reading. Thousands of secularly minded people who would never enter a church have read *The Case for Christianity* and have had, for the first time in their lives, the experience of submitting their minds to the gospel as an intelligent and intelligible alternative to futility in this century.

What C. S. Lewis has done others can do, for the field is open and unencumbered. Many can develop skill in writing what is acceptable to magazines. In this work the principle to remember is that the missionary task is best accomplished through the medium of secular magazines. Good as the *Christian Century* is, it is far more important for a concerned Christian to place an article in the *Reader's Digest* or the *Atlantic Monthly* than in the *Christian Century.* Too often we waste our energy by convincing the already convinced.

5. *The fifth minimum criterion of membership is the loyal acceptance of discipline.* This is so large a matter that it requires a chapter of its own. To this we accordingly turn in the chapter immediately following.

Chapter IV

THE RECOVERY OF DISCIPLINE

> *The flourishing and decaying of all civil societies, all the moments and turnings of human occasions are moved to and fro upon the axle of discipline.*
>
> —JOHN MILTON

During the recent war, with its uprooting of the life of millions, both civil and military, those who had most reason to be concerned with the maintenance of the spiritual life made an instructive discovery. They found that, in most instances, it was the people with a strict or even narrow faith who kept the best grip on themselves in the chaotic days through which all were forced to live. For a generation or more we had been moving, so far as the rank and file was concerned, toward a more liberal and broad interpretation of the spiritual life and this had usually been looked upon as a gain; but suddenly, in the time of severe testing, it appeared as a loss. The Orthodox Jews held to their convictions more firmly and more efficaciously than did the Reformed Jews; those of fundamentalist tendencies were more likely to keep up the practice of their religion in camp than were the mod-

82

ernists and liberals. Among those who held to their faith most couragously and firmly were the Seventh-Day Adventists and the Mormons, though both were looked upon by the general public as eccentric.

This experience during the war is now matched by similar experience in the almost equally difficult days of alleged peace, when the crisis is not ended but has merely changed phase. In our colleges and universities the liberal forces often count for very little, because they are so lacking in either courage or vigor, while some other groups, with not a tenth as many members, make their influence felt in a remarkable way. A well-informed and highly intelligent counselor, writing from a campus occupied by more than ten thousand students, presents this contrast in the following trenchant words: "Speaking bluntly, almost the only Protestant student group on the campus that takes its calling seriously enough to have a defined membership, articulate a position and pay the price in practical discipline, is the local Inter-Varsity Christian Fellowship. The kindly way of well-bred people who welcome all in their company who have a sense of humor and don't raise their voices when they talk— seems an inadequate basis of maintaining membership in a movement which claims to be revolutionary in its impact."[1]

This counselor's cartoon of the average well-bred group is not greatly overdrawn. The notion of making strict lines of distinction, of having a defined membership, is alien to our popular mentality. After all, we don't want to seem pious! And, in any case, we must let the winds of freedom blow. The end result of this kind of freedom is emptiness, but emptiness does not give people much to live by in a time

[1] *Newsletter,* Conference on Disciplined Life and Service, June, 1947, p. 7.

of strain. The more narrow groups, by contrast, may make some mistakes in the direction of dogmatism, but at least they do have something positive to unite them. They have something that sticks with them after they have been uprooted and transferred to army camp, munitions town or university campus. What is this that they all have, in spite of their differences?

As we analyze the experience of these faithful and courageous minorities we find that there is one factor which all have in common, *the acceptance of discipline.* The Orthodox Jews have the discipline of the refusal to eat pork, of the separate Sabbath, and of the specially donned clothing during the prayer. All this makes them a people apart, sometimes persecuted and despised, but the discipline, however trivial it may seem, is a source of strength. The faithful Roman Catholic has the discipline of confession, of early Mass, of the Friday fast. This last may be largely fictitious, since fish is regularly substituted for meat, but the very reminder is helpful to many. In any case, it is beneficent to have the ordinary Western rule of self-indulgence and doing what you please limited at even a few points. The Mormon has the discipline of the renunciation of alcohol, coffee, tea and tobacco, along with the far more revolutionary practice of giving one or two years in missionary labor at his own expense. The Adventist has the discipline of the Saturday rest and worship, often at the expense of ridicule, and he has the still more difficult discipline of giving rigidly one-tenth of his net income to the spread of the gospel. The Intervarsity Christian Fellowship often seems woefully out of date in its theology, sometimes being frankly fundamentalist, but it now flourishes on several hundred campuses, appeal-

ing to students and instructors of high intelligence largely
because it is definite in its requirements, especially in regard
to regular daily prayer.

As against these, what is the discipline of the Congrega-
tionalist, the Methodist and the Baptist? All of these had
disciplines once, but now they seem quaint and obsolete.
Membership, for these characteristic good-natured inhabit-
ants of the Western world, may mean anything or nothing.
There is not one unique feature that can be predicated of the
practical life of the average member of the Protestant
church, and there is very little that can be predicated of the
practical life of the average member of the Catholic church.
It is not a foregone conclusion that they are scrupulously
regular in attendance at *anything,* or that they tithe their
incomes. We have no idea what they believe on controversial
social issues.

The way in which we have sold our birthright is by secularizing, in order to achieve "success" or win members.
The steady secularization of the Y.M.C.A. is a case in point,
long noted by all observers, though we are now fortunate in
that we have a group of national leaders in the movement
who are seeking courageously to reverse the process. One
of our greatest losses has been experienced in our church
colleges, many of which are now more secular and pagan
than are the state universities. Often the most vigorous and
unapologetic religious programs to be found anywhere in
the entire academic scene are found in state institutions like
Michigan and Purdue, whereas those which continue to men-
tion their Christian foundation, in their publicity, are actually
disloyal to that foundation in that it is not taken seriously
and is not supposed to make a radical difference.

Originally the most famous symbol of the Christian college was the chapel bell, which called the students regularly to the discipline of worship, but this has been abandoned in two distinct ways. First, the chapel service has been secularized until it is maintained by opening such an assembly with prayer or Bible reading but often descends into a pep meeting or a time for announcements. It is sheer dishonesty to advertise such a gathering as a period of high and serious worship.

The other way in which the chapel service has been undermined has been by its increasingly voluntary nature. As an institution succeeds, it naturally attracts to itself a number of students who have no appreciation of its original venture of faith or who are totally out of sympathy with it. These tend to regard the faith of the founders as something quaint and outworn. Accordingly, they object to required attendance at public worship, with the result that they finally are exempted. Next, some members of other faiths ask exemption with the threat of withdrawal if their request is not granted. The leaders of the college, more eager for something called "success" than for loyalty to a deep original conviction, succumb to this pressure. Soon someone presents the idea that compulsion and religion are incompatible in any case and chapel becomes "voluntary."

The result of this is that the whole enterprise becomes trivial. Since English composition and physical education and natural science are required, while submission to religious exercises is not required, the students naturally draw the logical conclusion that submission to religious exercise is of minor importance. Being young they, of course, prefer an ice-cream soda in the Union to prayer in the chapel.

The result is that they miss the very experiences which they would never have chosen of their own accord but which might have been truly deepening if they had been under-which makes intelligent judgment possible, they have no rational basis of choice and thus the voluntary project is inherently self-defeating. Not content with secularizing our social agencies and colleges, we have done the same to the church itself. Members are eagerly accepted in order to swell the rolls and give an appearance of success, when there is no serious attention to either belief or conduct. *This way lies the very futility to which a redemptive society should provide an alternative.*

It is time to use plain language and to admit that our popular cult of freedom is a silly cult. What we mean by freedom is lack of all restraint, inner or outer, and we ought to be wise enough to know that no good life comes that way, whatever the field of endeavor may be. We ought to have known this all along, in view of the powerful object lessons provided by both science and art. It is well known that no trustworthy science is possible without the careful discipline of the scientist's hand, eye and brain. Indeed, the only satis-factory definition of science is a definition in terms of disci-pline, since science is obviously more than a body of doctrine. Science is a *method,* and the person to be trusted in it is the disciplined person. The undisciplined do not see what is to be seen through either microscope or telescope. The person without the requisite discipline cannot even read what the electronmicroscope says; much less can he prepare the thin sections which the instrument requires.

It is the same in art. All of us can look at a landscape, but it is the disciplined eye of the painter who sees what is really there yet hidden from most of us. Any man can pull a bow over violin strings, but it takes years of restraint on fingers and ear to make really excellent violin music when the same bow is drawn. That is why first-class musicians spend more time on what seem like dull exercises than they spend on playing finished pieces of music. The price of excellence is discipline and the continuance of discipline. The same holds true in the arts of writing and of public address.

Here, then, is our clue, if we wish to regain lost ground in the spiritual life. We should try to have the *right* discipline, but the primary requirement is that we have *a* discipline. Almost any rule is better than none. "There is not that thing in the world," wrote Milton, "of more grave and urgent importance throughout the whole life of man, than is discipline."[2] A few years ago it seemed to us that these words from the seventeenth century were an overstatement, but now we are not so sure that we were right. In any case, here is a concrete starting point for any who have become conscious of the futility and flabbiness of our modern life and wish to do something positive about it.

As we look at our historical models, provided by those groups which have been organized as orders or quasi orders, we find emphasis on strict discipline in all of them. The most stringent of vows within the orders for both men and women are those of poverty, chastity and obedience. That these vows are difficult to keep all will agree, but the consensus of informed opinion is that, in our generation, they are pretty fully kept. The vow of chastity, when interpreted as complete celibacy, must be surpassingly difficult for healthy men

[2] *The Reason for Church Government,* chap. i.

and women, but there are thousands who have won the inner battle and undoubtedly gained strength thereby.

We cannot approve these particular items of discipline for an order of common life, such as the Church should be, since normal home life is central to the idea,[3] but we ought to be honest enough with ourselves to be *as strict,* in other and more suitable ways, as is the monk in his particular ways. Similarly, we may not approve the constant reading of the same prayer book, in which the disciplined priest engages, but we are not honest in our criticism if, in consequence, we omit disciplinary reading altogether.

The older Methodist discipline, which required abstention from dancing and theatergoing, now seems to most of us, including modern Methodists, extreme, but it is a grave question whether our way is better. We have gone over to the practice of indiscriminate dancing, indiscriminate attendance at motion pictures and indiscriminate listening to music. Our sense of emancipation, together with our patronizing attitude toward our more Puritan ancestors, is largely a pharisaical pose. We ought not to return to their particular negatives, but we are unworthy descendants unless we find a better discipline of our own.

The most colorful figure in early Methodism, at least in pioneer America, was the circuit rider. He lived a hard and essentially glorious life. The circuit riders really constituted a special order, not unlike some of the Catholic orders. To all intents and purposes they embraced *evangelical poverty* in that the annual pay of each was $64. Their asceticism was that of the unencumbered apostles, foot-loose to serve God

[3] The failure of the Shaker movement demonstrates this.

and man. The hard and disciplined lives of these men, renouncing both financial gain and other emoluments, set them free to do a great work, with a freedom which the libertarian cannot understand. As usually happens in such cases, immense energies were released and directed to a single end. These men spread the gospel; they ministered to frontier families; they established churches and schools; they made Methodism a closer approach to an indigenous American faith than any other which we have known.

The Quaker discipline, which was extremely strict for about two hundred years, is one of the best known in the modern world. Everyone is acquainted with the pictures of men in plain coat and hat, and everyone has at least heard of the plain language of "thee" and "thou," even though these forms have been given up, for the most part, for more than a generation. Was the strict Quaker discipline of an earlier day a mistake or not? It is hard to know. It is easy to see why the strictness kept a man like Walt Whitman from joining the fellowship even though he was deeply drawn to it on other grounds, and we can all have some sympathy with Dr. Johnson when he said that a man who could not get into heaven in a green coat would not get there sooner in a gray one. But, having recognized these difficulties, we must also admit that the older Quaker discipline was a source of enormous moral strength.[4] It was like high straight banks, which make a stream run swiftly instead of spreading into swamps. In the lives of John Woolman, Elizabeth Fry, John Greenleaf Whittier and many more the disciplined simplicity of speech, clothing and manner of life released energy for

---

[4] The same conclusion applies to Brethren, Mennonites and all "plain people."

social concern. We have now given it up, but what have we put in its place?

The childhood and youth of many now at the height of their powers in the promotion of the Christian cause were formed largely under the influence of the Christian Endeavor Society, to which they owe more than is generally realized. The Christian Endeavor Society, in its prime, made real demands upon its members. Each member solemnly undertook to attend regularly both the meetings of his society and the public worship of his particular church. Furthermore, he promised to read some portion of the Bible every day and to take some part, other than singing, in the weekly meeting of his society. Thousands took this seriously and consequently learned their first lessons in religious expressions through this medium. Men and women now in mature life learned to pray publicly in these simple meetings. Today the Christian Endeavor Society continues, but the popular trend has been away from its specific demands to the formation of "discussion groups" in which we are careful to see that no definite demands are made. Soon religion becomes something to *talk about,* and not anything as old-fashioned as vocal prayer or public witness.

The evidence is really overwhelming. *Powerful groups, for whatever ends, are disciplined groups, whereas libertarian movements end in futility.* This is the clear lesson of history, and it is not likely that our generation will provide an exception to the rule. The person who gets up to attend early Mass is more likely to spread his faith than is the person who, with exquisite self-indulgence, reads the Sunday paper all morning. The man who reads Scripture or prayers each day is more likely to be a revolutionary force in our civilization than is his neighbor whose reading, whether at home or on the train, is largely confined to that amazing symbol of our contemporary culture, the *comic book*.

It should be noted in passing that the concept of discipline is not limited to religious movements, but it is fully appreciated by a number of secular societies. It is, for example, the general practice of all major service clubs to demand absolute regularity of attendance. The Rotarian must often be amazed when he realizes that his attendance at the Tuesday luncheon in the hotel is severely checked, with full accounting demanded, whereas regular attendance at his church, where he may be a vestryman or other officer, is not even expected, much less demanded. If he misses, for some reason, the weekly luncheon of his club, his discipline requires that he go to another town to "make up" his attendance and keep his record clear. What church makes a similar requirement?

In this connection we dare not forget the amazing transformation which the nazi revolution produced, especially in the minds of the young. Often the discipline was beneficent, though the general ideology was vicious. Most of the transformation in character came directly from the group acceptance of discipline, including absolute regularity in attendance, faithful obedience in regard to reading and the cultivation, in many instances, of abstemious habits. We ought to be deeply ashamed if we make the requirements of our redemptive society less rigorous and demanding than were those of this essentially pagan society.

In this regard the new cults regularly outstrip the conventional and respectable Christian groups. Some of the demands made by Father Divine on his followers are really extreme in their difficulty, but this, far from being a handicap, is a decided advantage to the curious movement. Many of the cults demand of their members a separation from the ways of the world that seems to us fantastic, but they continue to grow.

In the construction of a relevant discipline for concerned Christians in the twentieth century we are beginning to be in the fortunate position of those who can profit from actual contemporary experience. There have already appeared several spontaneous groups in the Western world, wholly committed to the basic principles outlined in the present chapter and willing to put these principles into immediate practice in their own lives. Accordingly we have a considerable body of experience on which to rely. Though we are still in the pioneering stage, we already know, in some measure, which items of discipline are more productive of insight and which are less productive.

Among those experiments in disciplined living now going forward the following may be mentioned. First, we can be immensely grateful for the experience made available by the formation of the Iona Community. This is a fellowship, formed within the Church of Scotland, by ministers and craftsmen who spend three months together on the island of Iona, off the coast of Scotland, rebuilding the ruined abbey with their own hands. During the winter months all return to the mainland communities, where they seek to apply Iona principles and to keep a common rule. The membership is cumulative through the years, interest being maintained by the fact that, wherever possible, all who share the discipline attend a day of conference each month and "regather at Iona for a week in the summer to reset their compasses." The craftsmen are expected to enter into the undertaking with the same spirit that unites the ministers and to keep a craftsman's rule when they return to mainland tasks.

This movement, which started in 1938 through the efforts of Rev. George MacLeod, began with the recognition that something is desperately wrong in the life of modern industrial and intellectual man, and those most responsible for the vision strongly suspected that part of the trouble lay in the general unreality of modern life, which separates brain and hand. They believed, with the late Archbishop Temple, that our crisis is not so much religious as cultural. They wished to bring back the idea of the total man who uses both hand and brain and thus overcomes his cultural disintegration. It was for this reason that the actual physical work of rebuilding was associated with creative thought and spiritual exercises. We may remember in this connection that Francis of Assisi began his remarkable career as a new man by starting to rebuild, with his own hands, a ruined church. The summer rule of the Iona "order" requires a balance of physical work, creative thought and worship, both group and individual. The winter rule demands "daily Bible study and prayer, a plotted day, and some attempt at a common economic witness."

Though only a few years old, the Iona fellowship is now beginning to wield an influence in many parts of the West and not merely in Scotland. "Friends of the Iona Community" now numbering seven thousand, representing various countries and denominations, make a modest financial contribution each year to facilitate the new enterprise. The community publishes semiannually a magazine, the *Coracle*, and there is now available a book defining the Iona purpose called *We Shall Rebuild*.[5]

A modest experiment in America, dedicated to similar ends and requiring a similar discipline, is Kirkridge, which is slowly arising above the Blue Valley in northeast Pennsylvania. As in Iona, Kirkridge proposes to be not merely a secluded retreat but "a group of Christians, mostly ministers, scattered over America and now the world, who live under an agreed daily discipline." It is hoped that this may be one means to a larger end, "God's revival of the Church."[6]

The rule while at Kirkridge includes early rising, morning prayers, four hours of steady group manual labor and two discussion periods a day. After evening prayer begins absolute silence which lasts until after breakfast the next day. This requirement of silence until after breakfast is especially valuable in that it protects early morning prayer from the competition of meaningless chatter. It has been employed by a number of experimental groups, including those organized by E. Stanley Jones.

Like the Iona community, the Kirkridge fellowship extends to people living at a distance whose chief link with one another is the acceptance of daily discipline. An interesting feature of the Kirkridge discipline is the direction that each day include a half-hour of conscious devotion *before a certain hour,* involving the use of a Scripture lectionary which provides for the *rereading of each passage for two weeks at a time.*

[5] For a brief but succinct account of the community see "The Idea of Iona," *Christian Century,* January 22, 1947, pp. 108–110. A friendly account by an outsider is that of Walter M. Horton in *Can Christianity Save Civilization?* Harper & Brothers, 1940, pp. 225 ff.

[6] Inquiries should be directed to Kirkridge, RR 1, Bangor, Pennsylvania.

De Iona - see
"Common Ventures of Life" Trueblood p. 27

A third and still more modest experimental discipline is that inaugurated by certain members of the Evangelical and Reformed church, particularly in Ohio. They have published a pamphlet called *A Discipline for Christian Living,*[7] using as its motto the words of Christ, "For narrow is the gate, and straightened the way, that leadeth into life." This discipline grew out of a series of informal conversations between two ministers and was tested as an experiment in Christian living by three ministers, their families and members of their churches in 1944. Since then it has been presented to thousands of Christian people of the Evangelical and Reformed church and other denominations.

This plan involves the introduction of a pledge card, which is to be signed by those who are willing to try the experiment in disciplined living and to be known as part of a fellowship of such experimentalists. The pledge is called "My Covenant of Christian Discipleship" and reads as follows: "Believing that responsible Christian living is the only hope of our desperate world and convinced that I cannot know or follow the way of Christ, apart from a consistent devotion to specific Christian principles and practices, I hereby covenant with God and other like-minded Christians to accept and follow 'The Discipline for Christian Living' outlined on the reverse side of this card."

In this particular rule of life there are seven items of discipline, and a number of people among those now seeking to follow it make it a practice to read one point in the discipline each day, usually at the conclusion of family worship. The first point is read each Sunday with the others following

[7] Available at Commission on Evangelism, 2969 West 25th St., Cleveland 13, Ohio.

on subsequent days in consecutive order. It is hoped that such reminders will help to keep the commitments of the Christian faith continually in the forefront of the Christian's mind.

As we analyze these disciplinary experiments and many more we begin to note a remarkable area of agreement, in spite of the fact that those who are pioneering in this important field come from such different theological backgrounds. All agree, for example, in the importance of absolute faithfulness in both public and private worship, not as substitutes for reality, but as means by which reality is more likely to be reached on the part of weak and finite creatures such as we are. It is agreed by all that popular Protestantism has been in grievous error in minimizing church attendance in the supposition that it was thereby stressing "the religion of the spirit." It is the religion of the spirit that we seek, but there are some ways by which this is more likely to be reached than others. In any case, it is not likely to be reached by the self-indulgents who condescend to share in public worship if the weather is right, if they have no headache and if the preacher promises to be interesting. All who have considered the matter seriously agree that we cannot expect recovery in the spiritual life, and thereby in our total culture, unless there is a renewal of the idea that concerned people do some things whether they feel like doing them or not. Only by such means are athletes trained. What we are beginning to learn is that asceticism is a valid part of religion or of any other important enterprise.

Another point of agreement is the emphasis on solitude. It is the conclusion of thoughtful people that we need aloneness as much as we need togetherness, and that the good life anywhere will include some of both. For many, it is only in aloneness, when they learn not to be afraid of facing themselves without the protective chatter of the radio or anything else, that they are able to reset their compasses. Here we have the divine example of our Lord, who periodically "went apart," as well as the experience of all who have gone into the desert. This desert, of course, may be in some great city and not merely in Trans-Jordan.

A third point of agreement concerns silence, especially group silence. This may range from the absolute silence of certain organized retreats to the silence of a Friends' meeting, which involves always the possibility of spontaneous messages, rising out of the silence and ministering to the assembled group. What many discover is that a near miracle occurs in their lives when they experience this for the first time. They wonder how they could have missed it for so long. The sad fact is that, for the most part, we go along with endless trivial chatter and the drip-drip of pious cliché when we might as easily be experiencing the healing influence of group silence. What all learn who try it is that group silence, whether on the Quaker pattern or on any other, is markedly different from the silence of the separated individual.

A fourth point of agreement among experimenters is the necessity of social concern. The whole disciplinary enterprise is a failure if it succeeds only in producing people who cultivate their own private spirituality. There must be a constant daily touch with common life and with human need. Though many societies have stressed this point, few have done so more steadily than the members of the Society of Friends through most of their three hundred years of experience.

"Concern," which began as part of the Quaker vocabulary, is now widely understood by others.

Friends soon saw that the final justification of the fellowship was the creative way in which it led people into the service of their fellow men. A concern arises when the deep experience of the knowledge of God as revealed by Christ, and especially that knowledge which emerges in the minds of a genuine fellowship, leads those thus shaken to perform deeds of mercy to their neighbors wherever found. Thus the concern accomplishes the marriage of the inner and the outer; it joins, in miraculous fashion, the roots and the fruits of religion. Three centuries of the experiment have demonstrated that equal attention to both the roots and the fruits is possible and that spiritual health is found wherever this situation obtains.

Where only the roots are emphasized, we have a situation in which people luxuriate in their own religious emotions, developing their inner experiences for their own sake. It is easy for religion to stop here, but when it does, we have little more than spiritual sensuality. It is fundamentally self-centered. Where, on the other hand, only the fruits are emphasized, we have mere creaturely activity, the kind of worldly philanthropy which eventually is little more than professional social service. Friends, in their long history, have often made both of these mistakes, but the major tradition has been the avoidance of both by keeping the connection close. Worship of God is one thing and service of mankind is another, but the first is dishonest unless it eventuates in the latter and the latter is superficial unless it springs from the former. A realization of this has led many Friends to think of John Woolman as their best exemplar. In his experience, more truly than in that of most, great sensitivity to social wrongs stemmed directly from a sense of God's presence and sovereignty. The world is helped whenever any man or any group of men demonstrates the power which this close connection makes possible.

Each group which undertakes the idea of discipline with any seriousness must be encouraged to produce its own discipline, though the experience of many persons and many centuries will naturally be honored. The very task of helping to make the discipline by which the redemptive group proposes to live *and thus restore veracity to membership* is itself a potentially creative task. The experience of coming to "a sense of the meeting" in this important venture may be more fruitful than can be realized in advance of the experience.

The following *minimum discipline* is suggested, not as a finished product or as in any way ideal, but as a possible starting point for any group of concerned people, anywhere, who are tired of waiting and propose now to *begin*. Each point may be elaborated and probably some new points should be added. Certainly individuals will find it wise to add those points especially relevant to their particular situations, needs and temptations. The points now tentatively suggested are:

1. *Worship*. Regular and unargued sharing in the public worship of God is expected of all who would truly be members of a redemptive society. The minimum attendance is once a week, but may well be more.

2. *Solitude*. Each person who seeks to proceed from nominal to real membership in the Church of Jesus Christ must agree to spend some part of each day alone, in private

prayer or other devotional exercises. These may include the devout reading of classic prayers, the use of devotional literature, silent meditation and the reading of the Holy Scriptures.[8] In the reading of the Scriptures it is strongly advised that a definite plan be followed and that the practice of re-reading the same passage for many consecutive days be tried, until the deeper meanings become plain. Most Bible reading is too quickly accomplished. Frequently it will be desirable for a genuine fellowship group to decide together on an order of reading and expect its members to follow this order. Such acceptance of group guidance is often a valuable antidote to our conventional individualism.

3. *Silence.* Each person who wishes to be creatively Christian must learn the discipline of silence. He must learn to get his body still and he must learn to get his mind still. Apart from this the deeper messages of the still small voice will not be heard. In countless churches, services of worship begin with the words, "The Lord is in His holy temple; let all the earth keep silence before him," and then, instead of obeying these sacred words, the congregation immediately does something noisy. We say, "Be still and know," and then proceed to talk. It is not likely that we can cultivate the art of listening apart from silence. One danger is that we tend to become restless and make the silence brief. It is important to recognize that "a moment of silence" is almost worthless. Long experience indicates that an hour is required for the emergence of the best which this method makes possible.

4. *Humanity.* The concerned Christian must be identified with the sufferings of his fellow men and active in the lift-

---

[8] The members at Berea "searched the scriptures daily." Acts 17:11.

ing of burdens wherever found. The rule is that every day must include some outgoing activity, that is not for ourselves alone. It is easy to make this sound sentimental, but it need not be. Woolman's concern for the relief of oppression was not sentimental and ours need not be. This service must go beyond conventional philanthropy to various deeds of social action, in many of which each person can act alone. The extension of real friendship to a representative of another race, the lending of a hand to an overworked young mother— these are not grand or colorful acts, but they are the stuff of which Christian behavior is made. One of the chief concrete ways in which social concern can be expressed daily is in care for the reputations of others. This involves refusal to participate in slander and malicious gossip, which are such a temptation to otherwise good people. One of the most disciplined of another generation put it memorably when he said, "O how good it is, and how it tendeth to peace, to be silent about other men, and not to believe at random all that is said, nor eagerly to report what we have heard."[9]

5. *Austerity.* The tradition for simple living is more than a tradition. It has a double justification in that the rejection of luxury serves, on the one hand, to release the mind from worldly interests, and, on the other hand, to release income for the service of God and man. Many poor groups of concerned Christians are able to give to foreign or domestic relief in amounts which shame more wealthy congregations, largely because they live in such simplicity that they do not require all of their earnings for their private and family use. *Austerity and charity go together.* The reason why the Seventh-Day Adventists can give regularly a tenth of their

[9] *The Imitation of Christ,* III, xiv, 5.

incomes and thus provide phenomenal amounts for missionary work is not that Adventists are rich, for they are not, but
rather that they discipline themselves by frugal living. It is
not required of us that we reinstitute a plain garb or return
to horses and buggies, but it is required of us that we learn
to regulate our personal finances in such a way that planned
and intelligent giving is possible. The present practice, in
many churches, of placing the gathered offering on the communion table is not just a tricky device. It touches the reality
of the situation. All true religion is concerned with money,
because money makes a difference in human life.

Such a discipline is tentative and manifestly inadequate,
but it is so much beyond what we normally experience in the
modern world that it is really revolutionary. Imperfect as it
is, any group of concerned persons who will accept loyally
this five-point discipline, along with the principles outlined
in Chapter III, will belong to a new world. We need people
to discuss it, but far more, we need people who will *try* it.
Some consideration of the ways in which it may be tried will
appear in the following and final chapter.

Chapter V

THE GRACE OF IMPATIENCE

Work while it is day, for the night cometh when no man can work.

Our present situation provides abundant reason for both great hope and great discouragement. From one point of view the spiritual life of the West is glorious today, but from another point of view it is in full decay. The encouraging aspect of the situation relates chiefly to our theological leadership. Not for a hundred years has there been such able work in theology as is provided today. We have now the assistance of men of the greatest distinction in various Western countries, all concerned with ultimate questions and writing about them in a brilliant manner. No longer is it necessary to flounder helplessly when dealing with questions of the relations of science and religion, of ethical relativity, of prayer and natural law. These questions are never wholly answered, of course, but the point is that they are now answered in ways comparable to those employed by the best minds in any field of intellectual endeavor.

The practical result of this great work is that the devout Christian believer need not be intellectually apologetic. The reasons for believing in God, in the sense of One who has a purpose for the world, who is deeply personal and who cares for every one of His children, are presented today with clarity and force in numerous able books. Furthermore, the difficulties are honestly faced and no hard problems are avoided. In short, theology has recovered both its intellectual integrity and its virility. This is a period which will be remembered for its great names in the intellectual defense of the Christian faith, and it is probable that the name of the late Archbishop Temple will be remembered longer than any other.

Coupled with this theological vigor is the existence of the horizontal fellowship mentioned earlier. The people who share in the ecumenical movement, the men who do most of the preaching in our colleges and universities, the authors who write for *Christendom* and *Religion in Life*—these and a good many more present a heartening spectacle. They present a spectacle of genuine catholicity of faith and practice. They constitute a true freemasonry, an existential Christian order in immediate operation. The Inter-seminary Conference at Oxford, Ohio, in June, 1947, was an overt demonstration of the latent power in this group that has found union already. They constitute the New Reformation of our time, marked by a recovery of urgency, a sense of Christian union, an appreciation of intellectual clarity and a common sense of the missionary task.

All this is extremely heartening, but, as we pass beyond this level of concern, we have ample cause for discouragement. The ideas which are accepted without discussion or argument in the horizontal, ecumenical layer of Christendom are actually unfamiliar or even unknown in thousands of ordinary churches. There are many ministers who are untouched by the fresh new spirit, living in a different spiritual world from that which the Inter-seminary Conference represented. The tragedy is that there is such a hiatus. We must discover or create some means by which the New Reformation may reach the rank and file of would-be Christians or the even more numerous rank and file of the quasi pagans.

What is proposed in this book is a practical way of bridging the gap in our current spiritual life. It is proposed that real renewal of life can come by the building of living fellowships in the midst of our present welter of futility, perplexity and dismay. There is, we discover, a Christian philosophy of civilization, and this philosophy is represented by the formula: recovery through faith through fellowship. We cannot have general cultural recovery without a burning faith, and faith will not be revived except through redemptive fellowships which serve to crack open even the most hostile world. If we believe this is true, there is only one thing to do—*begin!* We must have a number of people now who will begin at once without waiting for anybody to give permission and without too much attention to the difficulties involved.

One of the most harmful forces in the spiritual life may be the counsel of prudence. Whenever any exciting venture is proposed, there are always some to advise caution. The giving of cautious advice is the easiest and cheapest way of achieving a reputation for wisdom, because anyone can qualify. All that is needed is the purely vocal ability to say, "Now be sure you have looked at all sides of the question." There are times, of course, when a degree of caution is really wise, but there are countless other times when it is damaging to the spirit of adventure which our world so sorely needs and which is relatively scarce. What needs stressing now is the spirit which sees the need and proposes to follow at once something that involves a promise of help. The awful futility of our time cannot be overstated; the worst thing we can do is to do nothing. Accordingly we require the emergence of a bold and experimental spirit which is willing to gamble, in our desperate situation, on a fundamental Christian insight. There are always difficulties in the way of any course, as there were in the way proposed by St. Paul or by George Fox, but we are glad today that these bold spirits were not balked by the fact that such difficulties existed. They could not see all the way, and they were aware that the feelings of some people would be hurt if they should persist in the intended course, but this did not stop them. There are times when patience becomes a positive vice, closely associated with cowardice. It is good to realize that, while in some situations there is a grace of patience, in other situations there is the grace of *im*patience. "A certain excessiveness," says Whitehead, "seems a necessary element in all greatness."[1]

If the argument presented in the previous chapters is valid, we now have some general idea of what the major criteria of a redemptive society are and of the minimum discipline necessary to restore veracity to membership. But now there come to us several practical questions concerning how to begin and what specifically to do. How do we transmute the grace of impatience into the formation of actual loving Christian fellowships? To such practical and detailed questions, prosaic as they may be, we now turn our attention.

[1] *Adventures of Ideas*, p. 138.

One question refers to the relationship between a redemptive society as described above and an existent local church. This question is important and urgent because many of those who are committed to this method of Christian recovery are already ministers or influential lay members in already organized and well-established churches. The best wisdom here seems to be that of trying to transform the actual church of which we are members into the kind of fellowships of which so many of us have dreamed. This may be difficult, and serious resistance may be encountered, but on the whole it is better than division within the church or separation from it. Separation is wrong, partly because it is so easy. To form a new denomination is to commit a sin.

Sometimes we speak of "the church within the church," and there is a sense in which this is a valid expression, but the obvious danger is the creation of the impression that there is a little esoteric group which feels superlatively holy and sets itself up to be better than others. It is clear that any group which actually looks upon itself as having arrived spiritually is thereby giving the most convincing evidence that it has *not* arrived. Probably the best way to avoid this impression is to employ institutions already familiar to people and then to proceed with the alteration of their functions. It is well known that the prayer meeting, long a stable feature of standard Protestantism, is practically defunct. This could be taken over, in thousands of churches, without causing offense but, on the contrary, actually inspiring gratitude. The prayer meeting could be transformed into a fellowship living voluntarily by the kind of discipline which gives freedom.

A concrete program for such a transformed prayer meeting is as follows: Let the people gather, giving up all idle conversation before entering the building which provides the place of meeting. One ancient man, known for his tender spirit, was gruff when spoken to as he entered such a gathering, though he was cheerful afterward. When asked why it was, he replied, "I begin my time of worship when I close my door at home." In like manner the founder of the Cistercian Order in England was observed to stand for some minutes with his hand on the knob of the chapel door, before he entered. When asked about this curious practice, he replied that he was a man of many worldly cares and he could not enter for prayer until he was able to leave these cares behind. Metaphorically, this is a possible procedure for all concerned persons.

A group gathering in the evening in this way, presumably in the middle of the week, should occupy, whenever possible, a simple room, largely unadorned and so arranged as to make the company a face-to-face group. Rows of benches in auditorium style are almost prohibitive of the spirit and atmosphere desired. There ought not to be any pulpit or any chair so placed as to suggest that its occupant is in a position of leadership. For many, the presence of an open fire is a distinct help and, in this case, the chairs may well be placed so as to form three sides of a square, the fireplace forming the fourth side. The fireplace helps to recover something of the home atmosphere of the first Christian gatherings, which were so small and so powerful. Ideally the room should be on church premises, in order to symbolize the determination to work within the existing framework and not separate from it as a little clique who have become emancipated and advanced.

It is advised that the group thus gathered in silence, each taking his place quietly and unostentatiously, should continue for about an hour in silent waiting together, except when the silence is broken by a message or messages. Each attender must come, not determined to speak, and not determined to keep silence, but determined to be sensitive to divine leading and obedient to any call. Above all, the members must not speak in order to fill the time or to keep the meeting from being dull. That would be absolutely ruinous. If there is an open fire it is profitable to keep the lights low or in any case not garish.

At the end of the hour some one member, taking the responsibility voluntarily and in turn, should break the quietness and begin to preside in what is essentially a meeting for strategy. It is assumed that every attender is actually or potentially a worker, an evangelist. Workers need to confer with one another and this is a prime opportunity to do so. Thus worship is seen not as an end, but rather as a beginning. It eventuates in work and service. A visitor, once attending a silent meeting, and being perplexed by the fact that nothing seemed to happen, was consequently afraid that he had made a mistake about the hour. He whispered to his neighbor, "When does the service begin?" The memorable answer was, "The service begins when the meeting ends." This is the relationship exactly. Worship that does not result in service is barren; service that does not arise out of worship is superficial and rootless. Accordingly, the conference on action follows naturally the hour of worship. Since all are workers, they must plan their joint tasks, which often include deputations to places of opportunity or need. Each person should be asked to report on his missionary activities

during the week, seeking help from the others when unusual difficulties have been met. Major decisions concerning
professions and other important matters should be brought
before the group, and group guidance sought. The development of the common discipline should be discussed. The
prospects for new members should be seriously considered.
After a half-hour or more of such strategic discussion the
evening should end. Absolute regularity of attendance must
be expected and all must resist, consciously, the temptation
to be part of the "audience."

Though this transformation of the prayer meeting is a
live possibility in countless congregations, there may be
some in which a transformation of the ancient institution
would be resented. In such cases, it should ordinarily be
possible to use another evening, and thus make it clear that
no competition is intended. By such means the danger of
the esoteric reputation may be largely avoided, especially if
it is always made clear that the fellowship is not a clique but
is open to all. *Whosoever will may come!* The only selection
is self-selection, determined wholly by the rigors of the demands and the willingness to accept these rigors.

When such a group begins to be too large for the reality
of this face-to-face experience, the proper procedure is *fission.* This is the method of organic growth in which cells
divide and redivide until there is a large and healthy body.
The ordinary membership of the church would, in such
cases, be the major though not the sole field from which new
participants in the fellowship would be drawn.

Many have wondered what ought to be done about the
present church membership, which is often so inflated and
consequently meaningless. The best wisdom seems to lie in

doing *nothing* about the members already accepted, insofar as a weeding out is concerned, but in doing much about the acceptance of future members. It is probably better not to take any names from present rolls, because there may be instances in which even the tenuous membership we now generally accept may be the means of infection by the gospel. *But we should start at once to demand veracity of membership in the future,* not begging people to let their names be put on church rolls but challenging and warning them of the requirements as well as the opportunities involved. We can do this by full acceptance of the idea that membership, whenever real, is functional. We must teach one and all that to join a church is like joining an army; it means the undertaking of a task and the acceptance of a discipline. Meanwhile the present membership can provide a rich field for missionary work. The very fact that individuals once became members may indicate some openness to a step which involves real meaning, providing that step is presented to them. *The major strategy is to turn the present church members, one by one, into participants in a truly redemptive society.*

While the nominal membership may be expected to provide the most hopeful material for the building of new fellowships, we must not forget the seekers outside. The more we analyze the current situation the more we realize that there are thousands now outside all churches, not because they are not concerned, but because they *are* concerned. They are already unconscious members of the Fellowship of the Concerned. Many have refused to join the Church, not because the Church has demanded too much, but because it has demanded too little. Their criticism is not that the

Church is too different from the world, but that it is too much *like* the world. The humiliating truth is that no Christian fellowship has ever truly *challenged* them.

The persons just described are potentially some of the most valuable forces in the modern world. They are frequently both sensitive and brave and they tend to have high standards. In many instances they are terribly lonely, greatly in need of a sustaining fellowship. To such the society we have described might come as an answer to a deep need. Among this class of people there are potential interpreters of the gospel who may be far more effective than are most of the conventional Christians of our time. It would be surprising if there were not Pauls and Augustines among them. We may as well admit that we are not attracting them by our present procedure, but we might attract them if we should be bold enough to cultivate the grace of impatience and convince them thereby of the virility of our movement.

There is also another class of persons of great value which may be helped by such an enterprise. These are the people who are loyal supporters of the Church as it is, because they are wise enough to know that imperfect spiritual institutions are better than none, but who constantly chafe under the present situation, especially since so much of our religious life is clergymen-dominated. What about this bright and sensitive woman, the mother of a family, who has a good brain and a restless vigor of intellect? Week after week she goes loyally to church, hearing at least fifty sermons a year, though the ideas of the preachers are almost always inferior to her own. She bears it because she is a good sport, *but she ought not to have to bear it*. There should be some expressions of religion that are not clergymen's. This brilliant woman ought not always to be the listener; sometimes the clergyman should listen to *her*. There should be occasions, and not merely women's meetings either, in which she should be a participator. For her sake and that of the many like her, both men and women, we must do something to break up the convention that religion is something in which one man stands up and talks to a number of others whose job it is to listen patiently and put something in the offering.

The most practical way in which this beneficent alteration can occur is by shifting the center of spiritual gravity to the middle of the week. In many local situations it is probably wise not to disturb the conventional Sunday service, which many expect and which some sincerely appreciate, but there is no good reason why we should fail to cultivate a more vigorous plant elsewhere. Our clue here is the midweek church night, already a potent instrument in some communities and full of possibilities in others. The midweek church night can be the gathering of the truly concerned and without the artificialties which have come, by long association, to be associated with Sunday. Nobody attends the midweek church night to show off new clothing or to perform a superstitious and therefore perfunctory act.

The midweek gathering of the faithful, with its common Christian meal, its serious instruction and its simultaneous fellowship meetings devoted to silence and strategy as outlined above, can be the point at which the church we have known can begin to be the church as it ought to be. It is often right that the faithful should not attend on Sunday, in their local church, but it is seldom right that they should fail to attend the power meeting in the middle of the week. A faithful member should often be absent on Sunday because he ought to be carrying on his missionary labors in other places. His absence from his home church on Sunday will not mean that he is escaping his Christian duty but rather that he is loyally performing it. But seldom can there be a valid excuse for absence at the middle of the week. He cannot continue in the fellowship of veracity unless he breaks bread with his fellows and shares with them both in silence and in words. He cannot be a real member unless he brings his decisions to the test of group approbation and gives his thoughtful and devout attention to the problems of his fellow members. Because it is so much closer to the realities of living and because it gets away from so much that is merely artificial, the fellowship of Wednesday or Thursday evening may be vastly superior to that of Sunday morning. But those who now see this and try to do something about it are woefully in the minority.

A practical question, often asked, refers to the use of pledge cards and signatures. Are these valuable or not? Some concerned people doubt the wisdom of employing such devices on the ground that they tend to formalize what ought to be spontaneous and free. On balance, however, there is good reason to advise the use of signatures, largely because all men and women are morally frail and need whatever will strengthen them. We need "incitements to do well," because we are men and not angels. For a great many people the signing of a modest pledge, especially when they are urged not to sign unless they mean it, is a remarkably effective aid to persistence. This is because they honor their own signatures. Even the simple pledge of the Christian Endeavor Society has been more effective than is usually realized.

What we seek is some way of escaping the vagueness of so much current religion, especially in membership. People who join have a right to know what definite requirements are involved and they need to know whether they are in or out. The signature does not mean that the signer has arrived, but it does mean that he is *definite in intention*. How compatible this is with the deeper freedom of the spirit is shown by the fact that those who joined the Quaker movement in the seventeenth century often stood together and signed a book with great solemnity.

If we want a movement that is not a mere remnant but something which really penetrates the rank and file of modern life, sweeping our culture as have other redemptive movements in the past, we need to have something of marked simplicity to put into the hands of seekers. It should be brief enough to appear on a single card and small enough to go into an ordinary letter. It should be so definite and clear that almost any literate person can get the idea. Here would be one possible answer when we are asked the question: "Just what is it that you propose?" One side of such a card could state succinctly the five guiding principles explained in Chapter III, while the reverse side could give the minimum discipline of Chapter IV. At the conclusion of the discipline there could be a place for a signature, preceded by some such sentence as the following: *It is my intention, with God's help, to live by the foregoing principles and to practice daily the above discipline.* All who think of themselves as belonging to the fellowship are advised to prepare such cards and to carry some with them at all times, ready to present to seekers.

Another valuable device, suited to our finite and forgetful

character, is the use of queries. The value of the query is that it stirs up some attempt at an answer. A sentence in the indicative often produces no response, because no response seems to be required, while the imperative or hortatory sentence may be equally unproductive because people are accustomed to good advice. But an interrogation demands an answer, in virtue of its essential incompleteness. One of the most moving of group experiences is that in which one member reads aloud certain searching questions and lets each attender formulate his own interior answers in the considerable silence which follows the reading of each question. This is such a simple device that it can be employed anywhere, but it is seldom appreciated or used. Any group will wish to produce its own queries as it produces, ultimately, its own discipline, thus making the fellowship creative and thereby more genuine, but the following are suggestive:

1. Do you actually love one another?

2. Is prayer a reality to you?

3. Are you careful of the reputations of others, especially avoiding talebearing and gossip?

4. Are you punctual in keeping your promises and prompt in the payment of your debts?

5. Do you live in such a manner that you can use a portion of your income for the spread of the Kingdom of God?

6. Do you avoid defrauding the public revenue?

7. Are you sensitive to the wrongs and injustices of members of other races, frequently thinking of yourself as in their places?

8. Do you refuse to enjoy personal comfort at the expense of oppression and injustice?

9. Do you use your influence to help to produce a warless world?

10. Is your home a place where love reigns and where the Kingdom of God begins?

These queries, or others like them, can be put on a card and used frequently by the individual in the solitariness of private worship. They could be put on a card with ten questions on one side and ten commandments on the other. The members must be encouraged, not only to use such devices, which have been useful to other frail men and women, but also to create new devices of their own, particularly those suited to their special conditions. Almost any sincere Christian will be strengthened by following the practice of Dr. Samuel Johnson and other spiritual giants, in writing his own prayers at critical times. Dr. Johnson composed prayers at the inauguration of various enterprises in his life, such as the beginning of a volume of the *Dictionary*, the entrance upon the study of law and many more. Usually such prayers should be for no other eyes than those of the writer, but they may be precious to him. It is one way of keeping and reproducing high moments of resolve.

The theory of cultural renewal outlined in this book is by no means confined to a few thinkers or to a few movements. It has sprung up spontaneously on all the continents, bearing a multitude of names. Professor Walter M. Horton has reported many such tiny fellowships in war-devastated Europe and the writer has also seen some of these at first-hand. When there is so much spontaneous experimentation there are bound to be some mistakes, and we begin to see already what some of the chief dangers are. It may be worth while at this point to consider some of these dangers.

The greatest danger of any redemptive movement which stresses veracity of membership is the one already mentioned, that the resultant fellowship may seem, or actually be, a group guilty of spiritual snobbishness. The danger occurs to almost everyone and has been mentioned in many letters. It is important to see it as a real danger and to take effective steps to avoid it. The central way of avoiding it, of course, is for the members to avoid it in fact. If all are truly humble about their own spiritual achievements, conscious of their own failures, the danger is lessened. It is wholly consistent to have a high opinion of the value of the redemptive fellowship, believing that it is God's way of changing the world and truly the salt of the earth, and at the same time to have a low opinion of the talents or attainments of all individual members within it.

Even with actual humility, however, harm may still be done by the use of language that is not understood. For this reason it is better not to use such a word as "cell," even though the biological metaphor is excellent and though the concept, as employed in Marxian circles, is well known to literate people. No matter how attractive the idea is, we ought not to use the word so long as it connotes the esoteric clique, in a considerable number of minds. For the same reason it is strongly advised that we do not use the word "remnant." Though the remnant idea has a firm place in the Old Testament, and though it is perfectly clear that the concept involves the regeneration of all mankind and not the self-cultivation of a "Holy Club," the very word seems to be an offense. How offensive it may be is indicated by the following statement, which appeared in an early number of the *Coracle,* the semiannual publication of the Iona Community: "Any church that is content to be a remnant (ceasing to be missionary in its determination to spread the gospel to every creature) ceases thereby to be a church." This is true, and any language which obscures this must be discarded. *What we seek is the total penetration of our total culture by the total gospel.* Any language which fails to make this clear is a handicap. One of the great merits of the word "concerned" is that it does not seem to involve this handicap or connote the suggestion of the spiritually elite at all. There must be other words which fall into this category. Such words are valuable and must be made current.

Another danger of major importance is involved in the reference sometimes made to a "new monasticism." Those who use this term do not really imply a retreat from the world, but that is the way they are often understood. It cannot be too clearly stated that the reconstruction we need will come most fully through those individuals and fellowships which identify themselves wholly with common life. Some in our time, impressed by the medieval model, have suggested celibacy, particularly for the clergy. This is almost certainly a mistake. What we want is people who can live in ordinary family relations and demonstrate the beginning of the Kingdom *there*. The eugenic loss which the Anglo-Saxon world would have suffered, during the last four hundred years, if the celibacy of the clergy had been in general practice is terrible to consider. A glance at *Who's Who in America* is sufficient to convince the doubtful on this point.

It may be easier to be a saint without being surrounded by the persistent claims of little children, but the easier sainthood is of much less value. What we seek is not merely a fellowship of *individuals,* but a fellowship of *families.* It must be kept close to common life, with all of its heavy responsibilities and attendant opportunities. The fellowship must be *in* the world though not *of* it; it is not that of the monastery, but that of the market place and ordinary professions. The glorification of common life is a higher ideal than is the cultivation of the separated community, no matter how peaceful the lives of its inmates may be.

A final danger concerns organization. There are many who would welcome some uniting organization of all the scattered individuals who are looking for an order roughly similar to that described herein. Consequently it would not be very difficult to start such an organization, establish headquarters, elect officers and publish a magazine. But this would be a grievous mistake. Some, rather than others, would be included, on the purely arbitrary basis that they had happened to learn of the enterprise. The organization could not be truly inclusive and might be actually divisive. Furthermore, a good deal of effort would be expended in the very formation of the organization and this would be stolen from the main job, which is that of the building of actual local fellowships. There is something deadly about the election of officers, partly because it gives the impression that something has been accomplished. In the fresh burst of life we are trying to describe there ought not to be any "leaders." The *Führer prinzip* is always wrong.

Having said this, we must go on to say that those who want something definite have a valid point. They are afraid that the fresh Christian movements of our time will be confined to bursts of enthusiasm. They do not see how a wholly fluid fellowship will ever be effective; it needs structure; it needs backbone. They are right; no invertebrate movement ever succeeds, but the way to provide backbone is not to elect officers; the way to provide backbone is to insist on the *discipline*. If there could grow up fellowship groups all over the world, differing somewhat in creed and in social emphasis but united everywhere by a common discipline, it would be a genuine order, even though it would not have a name and would not be noticed in the Encyclopaedia. Here is the way to secure definiteness without bureaucracy, and order without organization.

There may be other dangers in addition to these, and, if so, they must be faced, but the major mood dare not be that of caution. We must not wait so long for the development of a perfect system that we end by doing nothing at all. Here, as in so many other areas of experience, the abstract best may be the real enemy of the concrete possible good. After we have been as wise as we know how to be, the time comes when we must *start*. There is, in our tradition, a glorious warrant for those who propose to go farther "without tarrying for any."

What most of us now require is a new vision of God's purpose for mankind and our part in it. Before the burst of new life which we associate with the career of George Fox in 1652, a burst which we have seen as an encouragement for us in our own perplexed time, young Fox had such a vision. He was on a small mountain, in the west of England, called Pendle Hill. His experience there was interpreted by William Penn in a wholly ecumenical manner. Penn said that Fox "had a vision of the great work of God in the earth, and of the way that he was to go forth to begin it." This is precisely the vision which each one of us craves for himself. Fox, as Penn interpreted him, was not thinking merely of those who might belong to a sect of his but of all men everywhere, made in God's image even though they knew it not. "He saw people as thick as motes in the sun, that should in time be brought home to the Lord; that there might be but one shepherd and one sheepfold in all the earth."

This is the ecumenical ideal; this is the Christian ideal. At this juncture of history it seems far from realization, but it is eternally valid. This is the clear vision which makes us know how imperfect our present condition is. Perhaps it is the vision without which a people will perish.

What we seek, then, is the emergence of the true Church, the company of loving souls, exhibiting the mind of Christ. Our fondest hope is that our own modest experiments may facilitate the emergence of this sacred fellowship. We do not seek to make all men like ourselves. What we desire is that all men be brought into a far more ideal society than any we have known. If any particular fellowship ever helps to usher in that larger and more ideal society, it will have done its peculiar work. What we seek is not, therefore, merely our own perpetuation, but the fellowship of one Shepherd and one sheepfold. But, since *that* fellowship is still in the making, our modest testimony continues to be needed. The best thing we can do for the modern world is to demonstrate to all that a Fellowship of the Concerned is actually a live possibility. Modern man needs help in keeping alive the faith in this possibility.

Most schemes in the world seem unreal insofar as the modest individual is concerned. We read about our world decay and then, when we have finished, we feel helpless. Every person seems frustrated by the complexity of the modern world. We must find some place to start. It is precisely this which is herein proposed as an Alternative to Futility. If Jesus is right, if the redemptive fellowship is really the salt of the earth, here is a place where each humble person can begin, no matter how frustrating the world complexity may seem. Here is truly a place to start on a job matched to our size. No one can stop us in our effort to form disciplined and loving fellowships, beginning in our own homes. We have, in this undertaking, an effective antidote to discouragement in the realization that we are not working alone in our human power. The plan of world regeneration we are seeking to follow is not the result of human ingenuity but is part of the expressed purpose of the Son of God. Our planet may experience a real catastrophe and millions may die before their time, but it will still be God's world and His ultimate victory is assured. Even if another war comes, and civilization is more nearly destroyed than it now is, we, if we are still alive, can proceed with the Christian formula for world renewal.

We need not despise any effort, no matter how secular, which aims at world reconstruction, but we are very sure concerning what the primary and central need is. We need a new sense of life's meaning to end our mood of futility, and this comes only by a saving faith. The faith, in turn, is nurtured by a special kind of fellowship in which Christ himself is the central member. It is our holy privilege to help to nourish such fellowships. If enough persons do the same, we shall have a new world.

4/11/48